The Kanga

The Ultimate Kang

Kangal dog care, costs, feeding, grooming, health and training all included.

by

Matthew Burston

Dog Lover and Dog Owner

Published by: IMB Publishing

Table of Contents

Foreword

Pets are faithful companions that accompany you through thick and thin for as long as the friendship lasts. They are silent, yet understanding. They are intelligent, yet subservient to you. They become a major portion of your life once the initial days are over.

Among the animals usually taken in as pets, dogs constitute a rather impressive majority. After all, they are man's best friend! There are over 100 different breeds of dogs with distinguishably different characteristics and features that endear them to their owners.

This book focuses on one such breed – the Kangal dog. Like every other breed, they are pretty unique. A thorough research beforehand can prepare you for the challenges that lie ahead as the owner of a Kangal dog.

Here is all you need to know about the Kangal dog. Keep reading to find out everything about this remarkable species so you can help it transition into your home easily. After all, they are to be loved!

I absolutely love my Kangal, we have a tremendous amount of fun together. He is a happy dog and I am a happy dog owner. That's what its all about!

Chapter 1: Introduction

There is nothing like a trustworthy companion who shares a deep-rooted emotional bond with you. It feels good to be around an immaculate soul that exhibits a positive aura, irrespective of what your state of mind is. For most people, such companions are found in the form of pets.

Their soft, furry, hairy or feathery coats/bodies offer an amiable touch. Their obedience endears them as beings you can care for. On the whole, it is a mutually beneficial contract between the owner and the pet, which gradually transforms into a memorable bond.

People may choose different animals to have as pets. However, the most common choice is dogs. What makes them so special? Keep reading to find out!

1) Why Dogs are a Man's Best Friend:

About 43 million homes in the United States are recorded to have pet dogs. The statistics of the United Kingdom are also impressive – about 8.5 million households in the UK have pet dogs. Needless to say, it is definitely a preferred animal for a pet. However, different owners tend to explain their preferences differently.

Dogs are one of the most faithful pets. Even history holds evidence about their dedication and attachment with their masters. There are quite a few remarkable stories about how and what dogs did to protect their owners and how they grieved their loss.

For instance, a German shepherd by the name of Capitan grieved by his master's grave for six years! An Akita dog by the name of Hachiko in Japan offers another remarkable story about loyalty and bonding. In fact, the story was later adapted by a production house and transformed into a movie by the same name. A dog statue still stands at Shibuya Station (Japan) to commemorate the canine's love, sincerity and association.

That said, no more evidence needs to be given to substantiate how or why dogs are such loyal companions. It is almost as though faithfulness and loyalty is built into their genetic code and these characteristics are transferred from generation to generation.

So if you are planning on getting a pet, try getting a dog. It will not only keep you entertained but also will remain steady by your side at all times. What more could you ask for?

2) The Kangal's Secret

Please understand that much of the content written in this book can be applied to every dog, because when it comes right down to it, a dog is a dog no matter what size, shape, colour, price tag or fancy breed name we humans might attribute to them.

Every dog has a uniquely wonderful set of gifts to share with their human counterparts, if only us humans would listen.

They "tell" us when they are unhappy, when they are bored, when they are under-exercised, yet often we do not pay attention, or we just think they are being badly behaved.

Many humans today are deciding to have dogs, instead of children, and then attempting to manipulate their dogs into being small (or large) fur children. This is having a seriously detrimental effect upon the health and behaviour of our canine companions.

In order to be the best guardians for our dogs, we humans need to have a better understanding of what our dogs need from us, rather than what we need from them, so that they can live in safety and harmony within our human environment.

Sadly, many of us humans are not well equipped to give our dogs what they really need and that is why there are so many homeless, abandoned and frustrated dogs.

As a professional dog whisperer who is challenged with the task of finding amicable solutions for canine/human relationships that have gone bad, once the humans understand what needs to be changed, almost every stressful canine/human relationship can be turned into a happy ever after.

The sad part is that many humans are simply not willing to do the work and devote the time necessary to ensuring that their dog's needs are met.

Almost all canine problems are a direct result of ignorance or unwillingness on the part of the canine guardian to learn what the dog truly needs. Forget about the breed for the moment, because what the dog needs to be a happy and well-balanced family member has nothing to do with size, shape, colour or breed.

First and foremost, our dogs need to be respected for their unique canine qualities.

For millennia, the dog has been considered *"Man's best friend"*, and in today's society, when we want to do the best by our canine companions and create a harmonious relationship, we humans need to spend more time receiving the proper training to learn how man can be a dog's best friend.

A Kangal is a dog and therefore can be "Man's best friend" providing that the human guardian gains the knowledge they need in order to create a happy environment for the dog.

That's the secret: if the human treats the dog well and understands what the dog needs, the dog will be happy and the owner will be happy. This applies to any dog, whether a Kangal or any other breed. It is absolutely true that *"With the proper training, Man can learn to be dog's best friend."*

Chapter 2: The Kangal Dog – Brief Background

There are almost 500 distinct dog breeds existing today. People have bred dogs selectively for thousands of years – at times within the same ancestral lines and sometimes by mixing different breeds. This has created a vast gene pool for dogs – one of the largest for any mammal.

They are generally classified into five categories; companion dogs, guard dogs, hunting dogs, herding dogs and working dogs. This classification is done on the basis of characteristics seen consistently across certain dog breeds. Even within these categories, massive variations can be observed.

The following few pages will give you a brief background on the specifications of the Kangal breed. So if you are planning on getting a Kangal dog as a pet, this information will come in handy when you make the decision.

1) Some Facts about the Kangal Dog

The Kangal breed is a livestock guardian dog that is believed to have originated from the Kangal district in Sivas, Turkey.

They have an extremely protective nature. Whatever you entrust to a Kangal dog, it considers it as "flock" and protects it from all kinds of dangers. It fends away threats from wolves, bears, jackals and other intruders. For this reason, it is often used to protect livestock like sheep herds. It can nevertheless be taught how to adapt to the human environment in much the same way.

They are magnanimous in the literal sense. The Kangal puppies are larger than most other breeds and tend to grow quickly. A fully-grown Kangal dog is likely to become very large. You therefore need to plan your acquisition intelligently. If you have the space to accommodate a dog roughly your own size (or even larger), only then should you proceed with the purchase of a Kangal dog/puppy.

The Kangal dog needs activity to keep it occupied or it tends to become quite destructive. A bored Kangal dog is almost synonymous to massive devastation. Either entrust it with a job to protect someone or something or keep it busy with games, people and activities. You do not want to leave it unattended at home with a fortified energy reserve, or you may come back to a bewildering vision of destruction at its best.

They are likely to chase whatever or whomever it sees as a threat. It can be stray animals or some unknown guests on your property. So it is best if you do not leave your pet unleashed on the grounds. Also, you will need to install high and sturdy fencing to prevent it from leaving the premises. As said previously, it has a protective nature. You will need to put it through extensive training to make sure it understands "threat" as effectively as you do.

The Kangal dog likes to dig holes, tunnels and caverns – everything that involves clawing at the soil. So if, by any chance, you are as much of a nature lover as an animal lover, you might want to keep it away from your personal garden. The Kangal dog does not take competition for your attention very nicely.

They are noisy beasts, especially during the nighttime. For the first few days, getting accustomed to their barks and roars in the middle of the night can be quite disturbing. If you live in a fine neighbourhood, this might raise quite a few eyebrows about what the Kangal dog is doing in a sophisticated society. This can prove to be quite a handful until the time the Kangal eventually settles down. Even so, if it hears a "foreign" sound at any time during the night, it is likely to start off without any consideration for your reputation or the neighbourhood!

The food and medical concerns for the Kangal dog are more or less the same as for other dogs that you would love to care for. However, it's massive size does play a role. This might mean significantly higher costs of nutrition once it hits maturity. You will need to keep a close eye on its food to ensure it stays healthy and fit for a long time.

2) History of the Breed

The Kangal dog has a long standing history of being a patient, faithful and protective companion for its owners. As mentioned previously, its roots can be traced back to the Sivas province of Turkey. It has served a remarkable portion of its life as a guardian for livestock. It is still celebrated for the same traits for its owners.

The Kangal dog has a striking similarity with the Anatolian Shepherd dog – both are based in different regions of Turkey. For this reason, the names are often used interchangeably and the Kangal breed was not given the status of a distinctive breed.

However, the beginning of the year 2012 and 2013 saw the Kangal breed being officially recognized as a distinctive breed by a number of clubs all over the world – including the Australian National Kennel Council, the United Kingdom Kennel Club and the United Kennel Club.

For this reason, extensive documents about its history and origin cannot be located. Nevertheless, the earliest record that points towards the presence of Kangal dogs can be traced back to the early 17th century.

A famous traveller – Mehmed Zilli, also popularly known by the name of Evliya Celebi – notes that certain ceremonial parades were conducted by the Ottoman Empire in which guardian dogs (the Kangal dogs) were displayed in full fervour to the general public. It was to commemorate the symbol of authority and protection exhibited by this species. This is considered as the earliest documented evidence about the not-so-popular history of the Kangal breed.

With time, however, this specific breed was taken beyond the geographical boundaries of Turkey into countries like America, the UK and Australia. This is where the breed was further developed through in-line and mixed breeding.

This is also the primary reason why Kangal dogs from different parts of the world may exhibit slightly different characteristics (covered later on in the book).

3) What Does the Kangal Dog Look Like?

Needless to say the Kangal breed has an impressive past. In fact, it's present is equally attractive. This brings us to the part where we describe this beautiful dog species to you so you can grasp the reality in its truest sense. Here are a few salient features specific to the Kangal dog:

a. Features

One of the most noticeable characteristics about the Kangal dog is its melanistic mask – also called the black mask. The hairs on the dog's face (and sometimes ears) are colored distinctively from its body coat, which gives it the look of wearing a mask. The pigment at work on this part of the body is eumelanin, which may cause the hairs to go black, brown, grey or somewhere in the middle of this spectrum.

The Kangal dog has a large head when compared with its body even though it does not usually stand out against its body. Its muzzle protrudes slightly to incorporate its face. Kangal dogs with narrow and small heads are generally disqualified from being categorized as the Kangal breed.

The skull of a genuine Kangal dog is slightly dome-shaped, being wider at the ears than the back of the head. On the front side, the skull gradually broadens to incorporate its muzzle. Too small or too flat skulls are generally considered as a disqualifying characteristic pertaining to Kangal dogs.

With respect to its muzzle, Kangal dogs usually have smoothly shaped facial structures with no abrupt corners. The lip area is padded and hence does not disrupt the natural structure of its face. Besides this, its upper and lower jaws are roughly the same size. The cheeks are flatter and the lips area is tightened.

It has a complete set of evenly spaced teeth with evident incisors to help it grab onto its meals. The equal size of its upper and lower jaw helps in formulating its scissors-shaped bite. If the Kangal has disproportionate jaws that inhibit it from biting adequately, it is enough to disqualify it from the breed.

It has a black nose and any other colours are not considered authentic for this breed. Moreover, it has small, round-shaped eyes generally coloured in brownish tones. Eye rims need to be tight and black in colour. Pale eyes or the lack of colour or texture in eye rims is considered as a serious problem and hence should be discussed with the veterinary doctor immediately.

Kangal dogs have proportionate ears that are triangular in shape with soft edges. When pulled towards the front, they should be long enough to cover the eyes. They are set at equal distances on either side of the skull. Alert Kangal dogs will usually sport ears held at a higher level to reciprocate their state of alertness. They do so to pick up brief sounds adequately.

Cropped ears are not generally considered as a disqualification, provided that the Kangal dog is imported from Turkey. Locally bred Kangal dogs with cropped years are disqualified from the breed. This is done to discourage the practice of ear cropping, as it is known to have no benefits. On the contrary, it puts the Kangal dog at a disadvantage and causes unnecessary pain to your pet.

It has a moderately long neck that is powerful and muscular. It is normal for the neck to be slightly arched towards the front. Some Kangal dogs may have rather thick necks. However, if your Kangal dog has an uncharacteristically short, narrow or heavy neck, it is considered as a reason for disqualification.

Kangal dogs usually have large and flat feet – the front feet being slightly bigger than the hind ones. The paws are generally rounded or oval shaped with well-cushioned pads and webbed toes. Its nails may be black, white or mixed colored. Dewclaws may or may not be present. However, getting dewclaws removed is permitted, as it is believed to cause pain to your pet if kept intact.

The Kangal dog's forelegs, hind legs and body reflect power and endurance at every inch. Its forelegs are generally stronger, larger and well angulated to help in the free movement of its limbs. The Kangal dog's legs are well boned to serve its purpose as a Guardian dog.

It has a strong, muscular and powerful body with a slightly arching back and well-sprung ribs. On the whole, its silhouette depicts a dog on a mission to protect its flock. And this is exactly the purpose it aims to serve. The chest is moderately wide with legs stretched close to the sides. Although the Kangal dog is generally lean, it nevertheless needs to have enough muscle to serve its role.

Its hind legs are parallel to each other and slightly angled at the joints. Even though they are less substantial than the forequarters, its hind legs help in pouncing and jumping up on its attacker when and if the time demands so.

The aforementioned characteristics are those that determine whether your dog is to be considered as a Kangal dog or not. In other words, it is extremely important for your dog to exhibit the aforementioned characteristics to be called a Kangal dog. Failure to do so will disqualify it from the breed.

However, there are a few features that may or may not be present in your Kangal dog that do not impact your dog's identity. For instance, there may be white spots on the chest, chin or toes. Some specific species may exhibit a darker coat on the chest and the legs. It is not essential for the Kangal dog to have these characteristics and they have no impact on its qualification or disqualification whatsoever.

Nevertheless, as unanimously agreed by all Kennel foundations of the world, the coat of a Kangal dog has to be pure with no brindled, spotted or striped patterns. It usually ranges between light-dull or pale-dull gold to a steely grey colour. Kangal dogs are known to have solid coloured coats and hence if the colours are mixed, it poses as a disqualification for the Kangal breed. This is one of the most important factors used to classify the Kangal Dog.

The Kangal dog has a double coat that is thick and dense. This helps in insulating the dog against extreme temperatures both during winters as well as summers. This also protects the Kangal dog from wolf bites and other animal attacks. During the cooler seasons, the Kangal dog is likely to grow hairs on its coat to provide insulation against the extreme temperatures. In contrast, it sheds this hair heavily during the summer season so that it can maintain its body temperature at the optimal.

The Kangal dog's tail is long, slightly bushy at the tip and, for the most part, curled. It is broader at the body and slightly tapers off to the end – the bushiness covers any noticeable differences at the tip. It is the same colour as the rest of the body coat but may have a slightly darker end. It is important for its tail to be in the absolute centre and not dislocated towards one hip – the latter is considered as a disqualification.

When it is in an alert condition, the Kangal dog curls its tail tightly to reciprocate its internal state of alarm. At this time, its tail may bend slightly towards one side. Nevertheless, it does not determine the authenticity of the breed and hence it is not something you should be worried about.

Lastly, it is important to note that despite its massive size, the Kangal dog is quite speedy. It can easily run up to a speed of 50 kilometres per hour or 30 miles per hour. It is therefore best not to keep the Kangal dog off the leash, as it is more likely to race off into the unknown and travel a long distance by the time you realize what has happened.

The Kangal dog is curious by nature and likes to explore surrounding areas. It is advised not to leave your Kangal dog off the leash in an overly populated neighbourhood as this significantly increases the chances of unintentional mishaps and assaults. You need to contain the Kangal dog in order to refrain it from leaving your premises. The smallest of distractions are sufficient in get it ticking so you need to be careful about where you keep it!

b. Colours

The Kangal dogs usually have coats in earthy tones – browns and greys. There isn't much variety observed on this end. However, the melanistic mask is consistent throughout the breed. Even if the mask is not completely black, it will at least be of a darker shade.

The colour white is only permitted on the Kangal dog's feet, chest or chin. White colour on its face is enough to get it disqualified as a Kangal dog. The ears are almost always black or of a darker shade than the rest of the body. It is not appropriate for the Kangal dog to be too white or light coloured. Dark coats are therefore an important indicator for the Kangal dog in addition to all other qualifying factors mentioned previously. On this note, it is worthy of mentioning that solid black coloured Kangal dogs are also disqualified from the breed. Earthy tones are considered appropriate for the Kangal breed. In addition, if the dog is extensively chocolate coloured, it is also disqualified from the category of the Kangal breed.

As far as the melanistic mask is concerned, if it is not very well defined, it is not much of a problem as the breed will still be considered as Kangal dog given it fulfils other criteria of identification. However, it is preferable that the dog has a distinctive mask on its face and sometimes on its head too.

c. Height and Weight

The male gender of the native Kangal dog (that is, in its homeland of Turkey) tends to grow to a height of 30 to 34 inches while the female reaches up to a height of 31 inches. The former weighs between 110 lbs to 140 lbs on average (50 to 60 kilograms) whereas the latter weighs between 90 lbs and 120 lbs (40 to 50 kilograms). These specifications are particularly rampant in Turkey – other countries seem to have slightly different specifications in this regard.

The United Kingdom, for instance, specifies that the Kangal breed found locally reach to an average maximum height of 32 inches for males and about 30 inches for females. Their weight ranges between 110 lbs to 145 lbs (50 to 66 kilograms) for males and between 90 lbs to 120 lbs (40 to 5 kilograms) for females. However, the dog clubs in this part of the world have not officially documented the average weights.

The United States seems to have identical specifications to those of Turkey. The variations are slight according to the environmental and geographical changes. Most other countries where this breed can be found now have more or less the same dimensions as mentioned above.

d. Life Expectancy

The life expectancy of a Kangal dog – provided it is given proper diet, medical care and the right environment that it desires – ranges between ten to twelve years. Healthy Kangal dogs are seen to live for up to fifteen years. Unhealthy practices in any regards are likely to remove a significant chunk from this life bracket. Once the Kangal dog has matured and aged, its requirements will change substantially. It is important to keep these transitions in mind while caring for the canine. The importance of healthy, well-evaluated foods at the tender age is even more pronounced than the previous years. Although, like most canines, the Kangal dog is likely to accompany you through one-third of *your* journey, the memories built along the way are sufficient to last you a lifetime!

4) Varying Physical Features According To Origin

The Kangal breed has recently been recognized as a separate and distinctive dog breed. It has been elevated to the status of being the national dog of Turkey. Even though its history is deep rooted and profound, the evidence and documents are negligible. This is one reason why this breed is characteristic of Turkey alone.

Efforts are currently underway to import and export this breed to foreign quarters of the world. For instance, the Kangal Dog Club of America is currently putting in efforts to import this breed from Turkey so that it can contribute towards the local gene pool. There are quite a few Kangal dogs in the United States but their variations or "adaptations" are yet to emerge.

One reason why the probability for major variations does not exist is the fact that the Kangal dog has a double coat and hence is adequately equipped for all weather conditions and climates. There will be no major adaptations to the region according to climatic factors. Their sizes and other characteristics are also less likely to be altered according to the environmental conditions.

However, given the fact that most Kangal dogs are taken in as companion dogs in the western part of the world, it is possible to see the emergence of an entirely different temperament of Kangal dogs. The pure breeds are likely to exhibit more or less the same characteristics as depicted by the Turkish Kangal dogs except a visible variation in their roles and temperaments.

The Kangal dogs were formerly believed to be closely related with the Central Anatolian feral dogs, Akbash dogs and the

Turkish greyhounds. In fact, quite a few similarities exist in terms of their physical characteristics and behaviour. Over the last few years, however, genetic differences were found when the species were analyzed on the most basic level.

Since the demarcation between these breeds is more or less a recent feat, it is important to take time in determining the true breed of your Kangal dog. Most people and breeders still don't distinguish between the distinctive Turkish breeds. Seek out an authentic breeder who can pinpoint the differences and supply you with a pedigree.

There are quite a few complications involved with the purchase of Kangal dogs. The topic will be covered in ample detail in due time.

Now that you have a fair idea about what the Kangal dog looks like and what you can expect from it, it is time to find out how to go about the purchasing process so you can take pride in being the owner of this wonderful dog species. The next chapter talks about everything imperative to the purchase process. Keep reading to find out everything that you need to know.

Chapter 3: Purchasing a Kangal Dog

The Kangal dog is surely an attractive one. For whatever reason you decide to put this companionship to test, rest assured your journey will be pleasant.

Important note: The Kangal dog can be a good pet IF effectively trained from birth. This truly is very important. If not effectively trained, they can become aggressive dogs. Buy this dog ONLY from a reputable, professional breeder.

However, there are a few things you need to be careful about while purchasing the dog. These tips will not only ensure you are getting an authentic Kangal breed (considering you do not have extensive experience with different dog breeds and their salient features) but also that you are getting a fine and healthy dog that will adjust readily and accompany you through the years.

A little time and care devoted to the selection and buying phase can yield long-term benefits. Parting with your companion is not a pleasant feeling and you would definitely not want to go through it time and again (unnecessarily).

Be choosy and critical about where and in whom you are investing your time and efforts in for a long, unfaltering and memorable association with your pet!

It begins with the search for a reputable, authentic and genuine breeder. Sadly, there are very few breeders that specialize in the Kangal breed. So this is expected to be the longest phase of your search. However, once you have pointed out the reliable option, the going will get easier!

1) Searching for a Reputable Breeder

Every person operating a dog farm or being in possession of a dog litter is not a reputable breeder. Before you go hunting for your perfect pet, it is important to establish where and what you need to be looking for. If you are doing this right, there are fewer chances your project will go wrong.

Remember, the breeder is pivotal in deciding how healthy or long-lived your canine will be. There is nothing you can do about an erroneous genetic code so you would be better off staying away from it! A genuine breeder knows how to breed the best quality pedigrees. So once you've found the breeder, you have already landed yourself a jackpot!

There are quite a few reputable Kangal breeders in the world. A quick Internet research will lead you to the closest one in your vicinity. However, be smart about your research online as it is much easier to conduct fraud online than it is in the physical world.

It is important that you check and double-check the integrity of the breeder – whether online or from a referral. It is best to make your purchase from authentic Kangal clubs or associated members only. Ask for their association/registration if you think it is necessary for it will help you identify fraud. Also check out a few references to be absolutely sure about your choice.

When it comes to interrogating references, never hold back any questions. It is not exactly difficult to conjure up references that will never say a word against the breeder.

Never rely on telephone conversations or those in which face-to-face interaction is not present. Drive an additional mile to meet the owners and to make sure the Kangal dog they have is what you would like to have in near future.

Never rely on a single interrogation. If you are willing to invest a little extra at this point, rest assured the outcome in a few years will be highly likeable.

Most professional breeders will require you to sign a document – a contract – before you take your newfound canine friend away from their premises. It is a normal procedure followed by most breeders. Make sure you have read the fine print thoroughly.

Most authentic breeders will allow you to return the pet in case it does not fit in with your family or you are no longer capable of caring for it – it will then be adopted by another family if appropriate. However, if there is no-returns policy, you might want to rethink your decision of purchasing the dog.

In a similar way, there are other factors that play a pivotal role in determining the authenticity of the breeder. There may be a few more hidden conditions written in the fine print. This is the part that you need to read carefully. You will automatically realize those pointers that protect the breeders unnecessarily. Deliberate on these points before giving your consent!

Do everything within your capacity to establish the authenticity of the breeder. There is also a list of questions you should ask the breeder before finalizing the deal (covered a little later).

On the same note, there are quite a few questions you can expect the breeder to ask you to see how serious you are about getting a Kangal dog. If you are doing it right in the first place, the probability of it going wrong midway or at the end will be quite limited.

a. Deciding the Gender

Are you going to buy a male Kangal dog or a female one? This is one question you should have an answer to before you approach the breeder. It is not really something that you need to think through extensively. It largely depends on what you are hoping for in the near future.

If you are getting the Kangal dog for protection, rest assured the male and female dogs are equally apt at fending off threats. Both are known to battle wolves and other animals in more or less the same way. In fact, both try to intimidate the opponent at first before using their claws and teeth. They are difficult to subdue, especially if the intruder poses a threat to their owners.

The thing with the female Kangal dog is that it is capable of reproduction (if you decide against sterilization). On the other hand, the male Kangal dog does not have such concerns attached with it irrespective of whether it is sterilized or not. This might also help you in deciding which gender you would like to opt for.

Generally, the temperament of a male dog is likely to be more aggressive and unstable than a female. The latter is also slightly smaller than the former. So if the size or the temperament matters to you – it does play an important role in terms of controlling and handling the canine – you can make the decision accordingly.

Lastly, if you are hoping to raise purebred Kangal dogs for the purpose of promoting this breed in your region or for helping other dog lovers in your vicinity to acquire this fine dog, you will need to have both genders. In this case, it is best to acquire them together at the same age so that they can get accustomed to each other. The probability for them to see each other as a potential threat or as competition for the owner's attention will be significantly lower. The Kangal breed is not very good with socialization. You need to participate actively with the adjustment phase so that all living beings – including other pets as well as humans – in your house can live together in harmony. However, once they have settled, there will be nothing to worry about.

So the bottom line is; the purpose of your acquisition plays an important role in defining which gender suits you the best. Both are equally ferocious and equally loving. If anything, both are likely to prove themselves as trustworthy companions. If not your personal preferences, then the last verdict lies with the availability of Kangal dogs!

b. Deciding the Age

The general rule of thumb says it is best to adopt dogs while they are still puppies. This way they can grow according to the rules and regulations given out by the owner and learn to abide by them. Their personalities and behaviour have not gelled so they are likely to "grow on you".

In contrast to this, going for grown-up dogs means they are tough and ready to take on the challenges offered by the wild. However, their personalities and habits will most surely have become permanent. They are least likely to adapt to your system and might always remain an outcast. Unless you have had previous experience dealing with this species, going for a grown up Kangal dogs is strictly not recommended.

There is an age in the middle that might fit your requirements perfectly. You can always try to get your hands on Kangal puppies that are not too young and not too old. With a life span of twelve years on average, you have a lot of time to adopt the canine.

Usually, the younger Kangal dogs are apt learners and hence adjust to their environment readily. Naturally; the sooner the better. Even so, there are no hard and fast rules except one – the puppy should not be separated from the mother for the first few weeks. The rest is all good as long as you are willing to compromise and adjust.

c. Other Factors

A major factor influencing your purchase is the *availability* of the dog/puppy according to your *specifications* at the *time* you are willing to adopt it!

As mentioned previously, it is a rather scarce species because it is currently in the evolution phase. Although not non-existent, there are quite a limited number of authentic Kangal breeders out there. The chances for all things to fall precisely into place are quite slim. You need to be mentally prepared for compromise on certain aspects while pursuing the purchase.

On a personal note, finding the right breeder is more important than getting a specific gender or age. If the breeder is right, the Kangal dog will automatically be able to transit into your house and your life easily. If the breeder is shady, then no matter how seemingly perfect the specimen is, there are chances the outcome of this association will not be how you planned it to be.

Now what is it that is really important to you?

Kangal dogs do not breed all year long. They have a minimum gestation period of about three months. The female Kangal dogs are likely to come into heat once a year. Moreover, genuine breeders are likely to practice pure breeding by identifying a healthy pedigree male Kangal.

Given these natural limitations, it will be too farfetched to expect the litter to be available whenever you wish to find it. The Kangal dogs are usually adopted readily as they are few and their enthusiasts are too many! A word of advice – the right breeder sells the right Kangal dog. Once you have the right dog, you need not worry about anything else!

2) Meeting the Parents

Meeting the mother and father of your new Kangal puppy can tell you a great deal about what the temperament and demeanour of your puppy will likely be when they grow into fine adults.

The Kangal puppy's personality or temperament will be a combination of what they experience in the early days of their environment when they are in the breeder's care, and the genes inherited from both parents.

Visiting the breeder several times, observing the parents, interacting with the puppies and asking plenty of questions will help you to get a true feeling for the sincerity of the breeder.

The early environment provided by the breeder and the parents of the puppies can have a formative impact on how well your puppy will ultimately behave as an adult dog.

Meeting the parents of your pet will help you get a better idea about what to expect from your association. However, it cannot be considered as a guarantee for a successful relationship.

If the parents are not present on site (or if you are unable to get in touch with them for any reason), ask the breeder as many questions as you can to analyze their temperament. Don't forget to ask about their health and medical records.

Documentation and registration papers are another method of analyzing the well being of your new companion and its parents. This will be covered in ample detail later on.

3) Questions You Need To Ask Yourself

Choosing the right puppy for your family and your lifestyle is more important than you might imagine.

Many people do not give serious enough thought to sharing their home with a new puppy before they actually bring one home.

For instance, many of us choose a puppy solely based on what it looks like, because the breed may currently be popular, or because their family had the same kind of dog when they were growing up.

Here are some of the important questions you need to ask yourself before you proceed further with the acquisition process.

In order to be fair to ourselves, our family and the puppy we choose to share our lives with, we humans need to take a serious look at our life, both as it is today and what we envision it being in the next ten to fifteen years, and then ask ourselves a few important, personal questions, and honestly answer them, before making the commitment to a puppy! These include:

1. Do I have the time and patience necessary to devote to a puppy, which will grow into a great dog that needs a great deal of attention, training and endless amounts of my devotion?
   The Kangal dog may prove to be more demanding than most other dog breeds. If you don't have the time or will

to care for its diverse needs, you might not be well suited to pet the mighty Kangal!

2. Do I lead a physically active, medium or low intensity life? For instance, am I out jogging the streets daily or climbing mountains or would I rather spend my leisure time on the couch?
   The Kangal dogs are super active. So you can naturally imagine what a laid back life will mean – for you and your newfound association!
3. Do I like to travel a lot?
   The Kangal dog does not like being left behind (especially if it is locked up in a small space) and will therefore make all efforts to get its frustration noticed – even in the form of obnoxious property damages. Unless, of course, it is put on a specific protective duty as it used to be entrusted to do back when the breed was specific to Sivas, Turkey!
   The sad part is, given its massive size, it is not exactly very easy to stuff it in a travel crate and drag it around an airport terminal.
   So you need to evaluate and decide if you are more serious about your travels or about your canine friend.
4. Am I a neat freak?
   Another way to put this question is; can I tolerate the mess created by the puppy?
   The Kangal dog is a heavy hair shedder and it does so all year round! Can you really keep up with the hair strands spread all over your house?
   If you cannot, then probably the Kangal breed is not appropriate for you. You should be looking for low-shedding breeds instead!
5. Do I have a young, growing family that takes up all my spare time?
   A dog needs a lot of time and attention. If you are too busy or occupied with other tasks, your Kangal dog will feel neglected. At some point, it may even give rise to behavioural problems!

6. Am I physically fit and healthy enough to be out there walking a dog two to three times a day, every day, rain or shine (and much more when it's just a puppy)?
   Try to be realistic while answering this question. Most people find it difficult to admit they are not up for strenuous activities until the reality finally dawns upon them somehow.
   The Kangal dog needs an active (preferably athletic) partner. Are you really fit enough to tackle this challenge?
7. Can I afford the food costs and the veterinary expenses that are part of being a conscientious dog guardian?
   The Kangal dog cannot be considered cheap. It is an expensive breed when it comes to acquisition, training and development, grooming and upkeep!
   An estimate is given subsequently in this book. Look it through and then decide wisely!
8. Is the decision to bring a puppy into my life a family decision, or just for the children, who will quickly lose interest?
   If it is just the children's decision, who will take care of the Kangal dog once the kids lose interest in keeping up with its needs?
   It is always better if bringing a dog home is based on a responsible adult's decision! That way, the association is likely to last long and be fruitful!
9. Have I researched the breed I'm interested in? Is it compatible with my lifestyle?
   Incompatibility will naturally disrupt the whole point of association.
   If you are looking for a truly memorable relationship with your canine, compatibility is the first thing you should be looking for!
10. What is the number one reason why I want a dog in my life?
    You need a better answer than just "I feel like it" or "Because I want it"!

Have an answer that translates into a lasting relationship and not just a short-term infatuation!

Once you ask yourself these important questions and honestly answer them, you will have a much better understanding of the type of puppy that would be best suited for you and your family, and whether or not it should be a Kangal dog.

If you are too busy for a dog, or choose the wrong dog, you will inevitably end up with an unhappy dog, which will lead to behavioural issues, which then will lead to an unhappy family and extra expense to hire a professional to help you to reverse unwanted behavioural problems. Please take the time to choose wisely.

If you have absolutely decided that the Kangal is the right dog for you, the following tips will help you to choose the right puppy from the litter.

4) Careful Puppy Selection

Although your breeder can often help you with selecting the right puppy for you and your family, you will likely be feeling especially drawn to one puppy over another.

However, there are other considerations. How you feel towards a particular puppy in a litter is also an important part of deciding which pup to bring home.

Beyond your feelings, considering other factors will help improve the odds of you having a positive guardianship experience with your new Kangal puppy.

For instance, being a little objective when evaluating each puppy in the litter will help you to make the right choice.

While some people become very emotional when choosing a puppy and will be attracted to those who display extremes in behaviour because they want to *"save"* them, it is not a particularly good idea to choose a puppy that may be very shy or frightened in the hope that they may grow into a happy, well-behaved dog.

Some people will delve even further into their emotional desires or needs to *"save"* or *"rescue"* and will choose a particular puppy because it has obvious health or behavioural issues, and because they want to provide it with a chance that they believe the puppy might not otherwise have.

While it is certainly wonderful that we humans have the capacity to raise and care for puppies that may be afflicted with health or behavioural problems, it's important that these types of decisions are not undertaken lightly as such challenges can lead you down a path that could be an emotional roller coaster of highs and lows that can cause problems for both canine and human alike.

While many minor behavioural problems can be modified with early training, it's important to be aware that the time and effort needed to do so will be difficult to predict and you should be aware that *"rescuing"* a dog that could grow up to have behavioural problems may require the services of a professional dog whisperer or psychologist.

Pick of the Litter

Generally speaking, when choosing a puppy out of a litter, look for one that is friendly and outgoing, rather than one who is overly aggressive or fearful.

Taking note of a puppy's social skills, when they are still with their litter mates, will help you to choose the right puppy to take home because puppies who demonstrate good social skills with their litter mates are much more likely to develop into easy going, happy adults who play well with other dogs.

In a social setting where all the puppies can be observed together, make the following observations:

1. When the puppies are playing, notice which puppies are comfortable both on top and on the bottom when play fighting and wresting with their littermates, and which puppies seem to only like being on top.
Puppies who don't mind being on the bottom or who appear to be fine with either position will usually play well with other dogs when they become adults.

2. If the puppies have toys to play with, observe which puppies try to keep the toys away from the other puppies and which puppies share.
Those who want to hoard the toys and keep all other puppies away may be more aggressive with other dogs over food or treats or in play where toys are involved as they become older.

3. Notice which puppies seem to like the company of the other pups and which ones seem to be loners.
Puppies who like the company of their littermates are more likely to be interested in the company of other dogs as they mature than anti-social puppies.

4. Observe the reaction of puppies that get yelped at when they bite or roughhouse with another puppy too hard.
Puppies that ease up when another puppy yelps or cries are more likely to respond appropriately when they play too roughly as adults.

4. In addition, check to see if the puppy you are interested in is sociable with people, because if they will not come to you, or

display fear to strangers, this may be a problem when they become adults.

Furthermore, always check if the puppy you are interested in is relaxed about being handled.

If they are not, they may become difficult with adults and children during daily interactions, grooming or visits to the veterinarian's office.

5) The Documentation

If you have laid your eyes on a specimen you would like to adopt, the next step is to get it home. But don't forget to check through the puppy's documents in your hurry to take it. This ensures that the dog you are about to adopt is healthy and less likely to fall prey to unpredictable or hereditary problems.

One of the best ways to satisfy this concern is to ask for AKC papers.

The American Kennel Club is a national organization devoted to dealing with all matters pertaining to dogs. From helping people adopt dogs to making sure they are well cared for and also free from genetic problems; the AKC is everywhere.

A reputable, genuine breeder will be able to show you documents from the AKC that certify the dog to be absolutely healthy and fit, especially in the United States of America.

If the person you are purchasing the dog from fails to provide any evidence or any documentation pertaining to the dog, rest assured it is a wild shot best left to those who can handle it legally.

If not the AKC, ask for other legal documents of value. At this point, what you are trying to establish is the genuineness of the breeder and the breed. The Kangal breed is not native to any country except Turkey. If you are purchasing the dog from a place other than Turkey, you should be able to trace the line back to the same.

a. The American Kennel Club (AKC)

The American Kennel Club was built in the early 19th century with the idea of maintaining and registering purebred dog species. It maintains records of all champion species present in the US. The motive is to breed high quality purebred dogs with fewer genetic complications.

Crossbreeding between different dog breeds is so common and (for the most part) unintentional that it has greatly diversified as well as degraded the gene pool.

It is difficult to come across genuine pure breeds – the ones that are best used for breeding purposes. If low quality cross breeds are used for procreation, the result is even worse as the typical characteristics of distinctive breeds are lost.

With AKC, the lineage can be traced back to a minimum of three generations – at times even more. For the Kangal dog, it should be traceable to its native city! This automatically translates into fewer genetic complications and hence a longer lifespan for the canines. Who is in a hurry to lose them anyway?

On this note, it is important to point out that the AKC does not recognize the Kangal breed in this name. You will be able to find it classified under the Anatolian Shepherd Dog.

As mentioned previously, recognition for the Kangal breed is more or less quite recent. Nevertheless, it provides a good platform to start your search.

b. The Kennel Club of the United Kingdom

If you are a resident of the United Kingdom, asking for the AKC papers from the breeder will naturally not make sense. In this case, the next best option is to ask about the Kennel Club registration.

The Kennel Club is the UK equivalent for the AKC. The good news is that it recognizes the Kangal breed as a unique and independent one. So you can get a Kangal dog certified by the Kennel Club of the UK and be rest assured it is the same.

The Kennel Club is one of the oldest canine clubs, known to be established back in the 19th century. Contrary to the AKC, it does not restrict its scope merely to pure breeds. Instead, it allows people to register crossbreeds as well. So you are well aware about either case.

The Kennel Club registration – considering it declares the dog to be pedigree – is a promise that the dog/puppy you are about to purchase is genuine and will exhibit the properties they should. This means less stress with respect to maintaining and caring for the dog. This also means the dog will be more predictable and less surprising!

The Kennel Club follows strict rules and procedures to get the dog registered. It mandates the owner to provide evidence of at least one generation prior to the litter in order to get the newborns registered. This maintains the sanctity and validity of the document.

There are quite a few dog-registering organizations operating in different parts of the world. Most of these have absolutely no regard for the heritage of the dog being registered. They might be offering services on a single call – without even looking at the dog being registered!

There is no value of such registrations. These documents guarantee nothing as far as the dog's genetic code or quality is concerned. Such specimens are likely to exhibit "abnormal" characteristics and may even develop genetic complications at some point. Controlling such dogs is a challenge in itself!

It is therefore recommended to look for valid certifications like the papers from The American Kennel Club or The Kennel Club in the UK. Once you have determined the heritage of the specimen and found it to be reasonable, you can proceed with the payments and transfers confidently.

Still having second thoughts? If you know someone who has had prior experience with the Kangal breed, take him/her along for a visit. A seasoned enthusiast with hands-on experience can spot trouble before most others. Once the specimen has been declared clear for adoption, you can proceed with the payments without second thoughts!

6) Assessing A Kangal Dog's Personality

How do you define yourself?

Do you consider yourself hyperactive, athletic or a workaholic? Do you like going on long, energizing walks in the morning? Or do you consider yourself on the inactive side; spending long hours on the couch in front of your television set sipping carbonated drinks or sugary delicacies?

The general rule of the thumb says you should get a dog that matches with your own personality traits. Each breed has certain specific qualities that define their personality – apart from the evident differences in physical characteristics.

So if you are one of those who would think twice before getting up to see what is in the fridge, getting a dog with a hyperactive temperament such as the Kangal dog is a sure recipe for disaster!

Here is an insight into the personality traits you can expect to see in a Kangal dog.

Make sure these are in accordance with your own personality to ensure a well-complimented relationship. The rest is all up to you!

a. Temperament

The Kangal dogs predominantly have a ***protective*** temperament. They care for everything and everyone they consider as their flock.

In case they are put on duty to care for livestock, they do so efficiently – often barricading themselves in the middle of the imminent threat and their flock. In case they are taken in as companion dogs, their natural instinct allows them to consider the humans as “flock”. They care for their masters in the same way.

On this note, it is important for you as the owner to establish your supremacy over your pet Kangal. This can be done in a number of ways. The Kangal dog ***dominates*** the flock as a ***leader***, and if you do not highlight the difference, it will try to dominate you as well. It is imperative to let the Kangal dog know the humans are not to be considered as flock. Certain training and obedience sessions will be sufficient to inculcate subservience in your pet.

The Kangal dog usually blends in well with humans, especially small children. However, it considers anything other than the people it lives with as a threat. This highlights its ***non-trusting*** nature. You will need to socialize your pet by making conscious efforts so that it can realize the difference between enemies and friends.

This breed is usually quite ***active*** with a ***massive reserve of energy***. If it does not receive ample amount of exercise – both physical and mental – you are likely to come across the dark side of your Kangal dog.

Although not ***destructive*** by nature, it may prove to be so if kept isolated in small places. It is therefore not considered suitable for slow or apartment life. It needs space to explore and play to tire itself. If not provided, you can be prepared for the worst.

You can never truly predict if a Kangal dog has taken offense about an intruder or not. It has the ability to pose as a ***calm*** dog even if it feels threatened. This throws the prey off guard and may therefore result in a number of unsightly and sudden assaults that you might not be able to fend off on time.

On the whole, the Kangal dog is truly ***magnanimous***. It is a ***large*** and ***strong*** dog built for the purpose of serving as a guardian dog. If you are new to petting dogs, it might not be a good idea to start with the Kangal. It takes skill, strength, energy as well as time to pet a Kangal dog.

Although not ferocious or dangerous by nature, it can prove to be quite a handful if not handled properly. It needs long walks on a daily basis to keep the destructive side to a minimum.

Moreover, you will need to indulge in mind stimulating activities to prepare your pet for threats. At the same time, you also need to invest in socialization efforts to make it amiable for people.

Handling the Kangal dog is an intricate job. Be absolutely sure you are up for the challenges put forth by this breed before adopting it. In addition, rest assured that if the dog is not disciplined properly, it might cause some serious troubles at some point – including assaults, property damages and others.

b. Age

The Kangal dog breed, as mentioned previously, has a life span of 10 to 12 years on average. If cared for in an appropriate manner, you can successfully add a few more years to your pet's life.

It is important to remember that the Kangal dog is categorized as one of the large breeds. It grows rapidly and impressively.

Its height usually ranges between 30 inches and 34 inches (considering both genders) but may come up to a height of 6 feet (or more) when standing on the hind paws. That said; make sure you have enough space to accommodate a Kangal dog in case you are planning to adopt one.

The general rule of the thumb says puppies between the ages of 8 to 16 weeks should be adopted. By this time, their preliminary value exchange from their breeders or biological mothers is over. So they are ready to move into their new homes.

If you have small children who will be living alongside the pet, it is best to wait for 20 to 22 weeks before adopting a Kangal dog.

It is not uncommon to adopt senior dogs. After all, they need a home of their own as well. While you might want to do community service by adopting an older Kangal dog, you should be forewarned that such a setting needs experience and tolerance to work out.

Older Kangal dogs are mature and hence less likely to adapt to a foreign environment. Comparatively, the younger ones work and learn well in almost all settings.

Nevertheless, a pet takes time to adjust whether it is a young one or an old one. Young ones get disciplined easily but old ones can pose a number of challenges along the way. Be prepared to handle them before making a move.

c. Gender

Both the male and female Kangal dogs exhibit similar personalities when it comes to their protective nature. Both genders are apt at protecting their "flock". There is no dispute on this end.

However, it has been observed that female Kangal dogs are relatively better when it comes to trainability. They are more devoted and committed with their owners compared to their counterparts. Some say they are more affectionate than male ones. So if you are hoping for a lesser challenge, the female Kangal dogs will be perfect for you.

More notable differences have not been observed. It doesn't matter which gender you bring into your home. The problem starts when their natural reproductive cycles come into action. This is when the gender actually plays a role. It is generally more difficult with the female Kangal dogs compared to the male ones. This is a topic for discussion later on in this book. Keep reading to find out everything about it!

d. Companionship

There is nothing comparable with a Kangal companion. These beasts are large and appear to be rather intimidating. Despite this, they are known to make the best of friends with human kind.

They are exceptionally amiable and protective about the younger lot. For some reason, their bonding with small children is a sight to behold. Not only do the Kangal dogs fend off all kinds of threats to the young humans, they also play around without hurting the fragile beings. It is for this reason the Kangal dogs are considered rather perfect for homes with small children.

The Kangal dogs' companionship with adults is just as impressive as with small kids. However, it is important for you as the owner to set the limits and have your pet obey them.

There is an inbuilt tendency in most dogs to think they are leaders and that they should be dominating all decisions. If you let this aspect embed into their behaviours, they will become quite a challenge.

They need to be trained to respect the human authority and also not to harm them unnecessarily. This is the first step towards the beginning of a remarkable journey!

On this note, it is important to mention that the Kangal dogs are not very appreciable about other animal companions. They will most probably not adjust well in an environment where pets already exist or where new ones are brought in to give competition to the Kangal dogs – whether from the same species or not.

You will need to put in significant efforts to make them accept the presence of another animal kind – a phenomenon popularly known as socializing. This involves taking the dog into foreign company while ensuring the discipline is maintained. It is a tricky phase yet rewarding in the long run, especially if you plan to adopt more pets in near future.

Generally, the ideal time to adopt multiple pets is when all of them are young. This is the time when they are able to build bonds with each other without seeing anyone as a challenger for your attention. At a later age, although it will not be wholly impossible, establishing a mutually shared relationship will be difficult.

e. Intelligence

The Kangal dog is an intelligent breed. This can be understood from their behaviours documented in their local setting as follows:

"A Kangal dog entrusted with the responsibility to protect livestock searches for a vantage point located at an elevated position. This allows the dog to look over the "flock.

During the summer's swelteringly hot days, the dog digs a hole in the ground and stays in it to fend off the heat.

The older Kangal dogs are usually the ones that train the younger dogs to serve their purpose.

If two or more Kangal dogs are entrusted with the responsibility to safeguard livestock, they will take turns and change positions to maintain vigilance over the flock.

Their attentiveness increases multifold as the night falls since this is the time the livestock is most prone to sudden stealthy attacks.

In the face of an attack, the Kangal dog will first put itself in between the flock and the threat. It will try to place the flock in a safe place before getting in position to attack the intruder. Although the Kangal breed is not ferocious, it can kill a wolf if it feels threatened or is attacked."

There is substantial evidence to highlight the fact that the Kangal dog is an intelligent breed. You can further help them in thinking out of the box by involving them in mental stimulation activities.

For instance, build an obstacle course in your backyard or even inside your home (if you have that much space). Guide them through the course without making any conscious effort to help them. Treat them with snacks along the way so they do not lose interest in the activity. It will not only build their thought process and make them smarter; it will also build their physical strength and endurance.

This sums up the Kangal dogs' personality in general. Keep in mind that the way the dogs are kept and cared for will also alter their personality. So if the Kangal dog was taught to lead humans, it will try to do so with the new owner as well. But if it was disciplined properly and taught to behave well around harmless strangers, it will transit easily into your home.

Kangal dogs are quick learners. They will quickly pick up the rules of conduct within your empire. They will also catch the phrases often said to them and associate meaning with these according to the actions expected of them. They will generally transit quickly and smoothly.

7) Records of Healthy Kangal Dogs

Dogs contract diseases, fall ill and need medication in more or less the same way as humans. It is virtually impossible for the Kangal dogs not to fall prey to any disease during their lifetime. Even puppies need to be given shots and vaccinations to prevent them from medical complications.

A genuine breeder will keep a record of all medical concerns pertaining to the Kangal dog (or puppy) you are hoping to pet. The shot routine usually starts around the time the puppy reaches the age of 6 to 8 weeks and continues more or less throughout the life of the canine – though the frequency is distinctively diminished.

Before this time period, the puppy receives all immunity protection from the mother's milk – considering it is not devoid of this right. The first milk – also known as colostrums – contains all the necessary antigens and antibodies necessary to protect the puppy from imminent health risks.

However, by the time the puppy hits its 6th week, the effect of these initial protective administrations begins to wear off. Thus, shots and vaccinations become necessary.

a. Shot Records, Vaccination and Other Medical Records

As mentioned previously, the shots and vaccinations become necessary for the puppy by the time it reaches the sixth week.

Generally, there is a combination of ailments for which the vaccinations are administered. This popularly includes ***Canine Distemper***, ***Parainfluenza***, ***Parvovirus***, ***Leptospirosis***, and ***Hepatitis***.

Occasionally, this combination vaccine – also known as ***DHLPP*** – will be accompanied by inoculations against ***Rabies***, ***Corona*** and ***Bordatella***.

The vaccinations are administered at your puppy's second, third and fourth month. Following this, the frequency is reduced to once a year for the rest of its life.

Ask the breeder for documents pertaining to the Kangal puppy's visit to the veterinary doctor. If the breeder fails to provide any such documentation, it automatically points towards the shady nature of exchange.

If possible, take the time to confirm the documents from the veterinary doctor mentioned in them – to be absolutely sure before you take your new friend home.

If, for any reason, you choose to settle for a puppy with no valid records, make sure you make a visit to the veterinary doctor at the earliest. Have your puppy checked for all major and minor diseases and also draft up a schedule for vaccinations.

Let your veterinarian have a good, long look at the puppy to identify all potential threats. Add reminders to your schedule for the vaccination schedule so that you do not end up missing out on it.

The DHLPP vaccine needs to be given on a yearly basis following its initial administration. Keep in mind that the diseases this vaccination provides immunity against are extremely dangerous and may prove to be fatal. It is therefore extremely important to follow the vaccination schedule stringently.

Apart from DHLPP, your Kangal dog/puppy needs to be vaccinated against a few other medical complications. ***Heartworm*** is one of the most common and most notorious problems quite rampant among the canine species, especially the Kangal breed.

Experts suggest you should get your Kangal dog scrutinized for heartworms at least once a year – preferably during springtime. If migration to a warmer climate is involved, get your Kangal dog checked for heartworms during the stay there or as soon as you get back to the origin. Heartworms are quite common during the summer season so this is the best time to identify an infestation at the earliest stage.

Hookworms are another major problem faced by most canines around the world – even those living in the finest places and born to the finest mothers. It broadly categorizes all worm infestations of the intestinal tract including (but not limited to) the tapeworm, round worms and others.

Hookworms have the tendency to become a notorious problem if not nipped in the bud. It is therefore advised to have your dog/puppy checked for hookworms at the time you bring it in.

Also have your dog periodically checked for any signs of hookworms. Although not known to be lethal, it can become extremely detrimental if not catered to on time.

Fleas and ticks are also seen to infect Kangal dogs as any other breed. You can consult your pet's veterinary doctor for the latest on this aspect. The quicker and easier it is to rescue your pet from these notorious pests, the better it will be for your dog.

Fleas and ticks are not exactly a major threat for your pet. Nevertheless, it is a notorious problem that will have your Kangal dog scratching its coat all the time. Naturally, it will be embarrassing to witness a Kangal dog that seems to be at odds with itself!

The aforementioned conditions and vaccinations summarize some of the common problems faced by most dogs irrespective of their breed. Whether you are getting a Kangal dog or any other breed, these are some of the medical problems you need to keep an eye on to make sure your pet can enjoy a long, happy and fulfilling life.

So what about breed specific issues?

It has been observed that the Kangal breed is more or less a ***problem-free breed***. The incidence of any health complications is fairly low and there are no specific conditions associated with this breed. The probability for you to come across a defected dog/puppy is therefore quite slim if not entirely non-existent.

However, Kangal Dogs may have ***hip and elbow dysplasia***, ***dermatologic musculoskeletal lipomas***, ***heart problems*** and ***cruciate ligament injury***. Some may have ***Halitosis*** (Bad Breath).

The incidence is extremely low, however it does exist. It will therefore be a good idea to get your Kangal dog checked for these conditions at the time you plan to take it in.

Make sure such problems are not embedded in the little one's genetic code – go through the medical history of both its parents. The more thoroughly you search for signs of problems, the more rewarding it will turn out to be in the near future! Seek proper medical records maintained from day one. The shots are necessary so there is no way these records will be absent – until, of course, you opt for a puppy that is too small for shots. Put all your curiosities to rest so you can enjoy a mutually beneficial relationship with your pet. After all, this is the precise idea behind the association.

b. Dew Claws

The feet of Kangal dogs are rather larger and fuller to support their guardian activities. This structure allows them to run and act quickly and fend off threat immediately! They need strong fore and hind legs to support their massive body and movements.

It is one of those breeds that may possess dewclaws.

The dewclaw is an additional toe attached to the canine's feet that never really comes into use. It is usually located higher on the leg – possibly midway to the knee.

The nail grows naturally and is likely to become painfully long if not clipped. It does not wear out like other toe nails mainly because the dewclaw does not come into use. It is not a disability or an abnormality. In fact, dewclaws are quite common across a wide range of dog breeds. The purpose of the dewclaw has not yet been realized. It is for this reason that most owners decide to have the dewclaw removed surgically.

Certain theories suggest that the dewclaws help the dog in attacking enemy opponents and holding on to their food – especially bones and other similarly structured food. This is precisely aligned with its role as a Guardian dog.

Others suggest that it helps the dog in clinging on to elevated structures – like the side of a tree. However, most owners tend to have it removed. It is important to keep in mind that the dewclaw – although apparently useless – does not harm or hurt the dog in any way. It exists naturally and hence is not much of a bother for the dog. Removing the dewclaw is therefore not mandatory for your dog's health or well being. However, if you would like to do so in order to improve your dog's looks, it is more or less up to you to decide.

If the dog/puppy you are planning on purchasing has had its dewclaws removed, make sure you ask the caretaker/breeder about it. Also seek medical documentation pertaining to it. The more you know about the dog, the better you will be able to take care of it.

c. Certain Physical Characteristics of Healthy Kangal Dogs

Before you get to the purchase stage, however, there are a few general signs of good health to be aware of when choosing a healthy puppy from a litter, including the following:

1. **Breathing** – a healthy puppy will breathe quietly, without coughing or sneezing, and there will be no crusting or discharge around his or her nostrils.
2. **Body** – they will look round and well fed, with an obvious layer of fat over their rib cage.
3. **Coat** – a healthy puppy will have a soft coat with no dandruff, dullness, greasiness or bald spots.
4. **Energy** – a well-rested puppy will be alert and energetic.
5. **Hearing** – a healthy puppy with good hearing should react if you clap your hands behind their head.
6. **Genitals** – a healthy puppy will not have any sort of discharge visible in or around their genital or anal regions.
7. **Mobility** – a healthy puppy will walk and run normally without wobbling, limping or seeming to be weak, stiff or sore.
8. **Vision** – a healthy puppy will have bright, clear eyes without crust or discharge and they should notice if a ball is rolled past them within their field of vision.

If your Kangal dog seems to be facing certain difficulty in any of these aspects, demand a veterinary inspection before signing the contract.

8) The Question-Answer Session

Before making your investment, you are allowed to ask as many questions from the breeder as possible – even to the point of irritating the dealer. It is your right to put all your concerns at peace before making the purchase. Be absolutely sure about the specimen and its quality so you can share a mutually beneficial bond later on.

It is always a good idea to read up about the dog breed you are planning to have. NEVER go to the breeder with absolutely no idea about what it is that you want or what it is that you are looking for. Trade frauds are really not very uncommon. Knowledge is the only thing that can keep you safe from it.

Do not give in to the allegations put forth by the breeder. Even if there is something you do not know about, make sure you do not make it evident to the breeder. If you do, it will automatically give the breeder a license to bombard you with lies and false claims.

Take time to prepare yourself before heading off to the breeder. In fact, it is best to get information from multiple breeders and a handful of their customers before making the final purchase decision.

Keep in mind these decisions cannot be reversed as easily as you would like to do if and when you realize the plan has backfired. Even if you are approaching a breeder through reference, it is still important to make sure all your questions have been appropriately answered.

On this note, it is worthy of being mentioned that all breeders are not operating simply to rob you of your finances or to deliver low quality canine-friends that fail to behave the way they are supposed to!

You might be one of the lucky ones to come across a breeder who is actually helpful in guiding you towards the selection. While it is important to keep your guards up and not rely completely on the breeder, it is not entirely impossible that the breeder will have some valuable insight for you.

Know what you need to say and when. Don't come off as a stubborn know-it-all or as an ignorant person. Strike a balance – keep your eyes, ears and mind open. Prepare well so you are in a better state to identify fraud when and if it happens.

a. Questions To Ask the Breeder

Here are a few questions you should definitely ask from a dog breeder – generally and specifically to the Kangal breed.

Quite obviously, the focus here is interrogating the breeder about a Kangal puppy instead of a fully-grown dog. It is sufficient to give you an idea of all you need to know. Any questions you think are equally applicable to the dog can be asked as it is. If there are other concerns on your mind, discuss and clear those as well. You do not want to enter into a dog companionship with doubt on your mind!

1. How long have you been involved with the Kangal breed? How many litters have you witnessed and grown?
The longer and the more litters the breeder has worked with, the better it will be. This means the breeder has ample hands-on experience and will therefore know all pros and cons of the breed. At a future date, you will be able to use this expertise to your own benefit as well.

2. Why do you breed Kangal dogs in particular?
Look for a satisfactory answer beyond the usual gibberish. There are no hard and fast rules to determine which answer is to

be considered appropriate or which should not. If there is a story behind this association, show your interest and curiosity about it!

3. How frequently is the litter expected?
Too frequent breeding means the quality of the puppies is being compromised. Too many litters from the same female Kangal dog means it is not being adequately cared for and is likely to face declining health.
Healthy kids are usually not born to an unhealthy mother.

4. Who were the parents for the puppy?
It doesn't matter if they are not present on site; ask for images and medical records for both parents.
If the breeder is able to show you pictures of relatives, make a mental record for these as well. These will come in handy later on while further identifying the authenticity of the breed.

5. Where and how are the puppies kept?
Make a mental note of the sanitation facilities, cleanliness, environment, availability of space and all other factors present on site. This is what the puppy is accustomed to. If you cannot offer something close to this environment, you can expect all sorts of tantrums from your Kangal pet as it adjusts to the new environment.

6. What are the most common problems associated with the Kangal breed?
Although admittedly it is a relatively problem free breed, experts agree that a breeder who has witnessed a minimum of two litters will definitely experience some problem or another.
It does not have to be a major health complication. Any information that suggests the breeder has in fact witnessed multiple generations will suffice.

7. Are the parents certified?
Have a look at the certifications offered by the breeder, if any. If

you come across the AKC or The Kennel Club of the UK papers, rest assured the puppy will be healthy and happy.
As for other documents, take your time to identify if they are actually genuine or not.

8. Do you have any kennel club memberships?
Most clubs have strict rules about how the canines are cared for. So if there is a reputed club membership involved, you can be rest assured the puppies will be adequately cared for.
This is not a necessity. The presence of membership documents is a plus point – its lack thereof cannot really be considered as a negative!

9. Can I see the medical records for this puppy?
Make sure all the documents are in order – especially those pertaining to shots and vaccinations.
If there are any other "special" cases involved, make sure you ask as much about it as you would like to know. Better to be informed beforehand about what you are headed into.

10. Can I see the contract before signing?
Take special care to read the fine print between the lines. Inquire about individual clauses mentioned about the transfer of ownership.
Make sure you have inquired about the return policy to protect yourself from future troubles.
Anything that does not seem right is most probably not so – either have the clause changed or find another breeder.

11. What is involved in the guarantee cover?
Look for pointers about a return policy, medical coverage, exchange policy and everything else mentioned in there. You need to be fully aware of the options available to you given the association does not work out.
The contingency needs to be planned before the transfer or you

will be left with no choice but to put up with something that does not meet your expectations!

12. Can I have references of your customers?
A breeder that shies away from sharing this information is definitely one that is questionable. Most reputed dog breeders will have this information readily available.
Take your time to inquire about the canines from these customers before returning to make the purchase. Witness the specimen with your own eyes and don't believe verbal stories – the latter can be concocted quite easily!

13. Do you have any records of participating in dog events?
It will promote the authenticity of the breeder. If the breeder has participated in dog events, it is most likely to be genuine since all breeders do not survive the tough scrutiny conducted by the event managers.

14. Do you have experience dealing with this single breed or multiple ones?
If the breeder is known to have switched between different dog breeds from time to time, it definitely points towards instability and inexperience.
Look for someone who depicts consistency. Breed switching is almost a sure guarantee the breeder does not know how to handle the dogs!

15. Were the parents of the puppy scrutinized for dog diseases?
Look for detailed records that include investigating dysplasia, optical health, heart problems, seizures, epilepsy, allergies, thyroid problems, congenital issues, and all other possible problems.
The AKC papers and the Kennel Club of UK registration papers will have enough information about the parents' medical problems. If you have got your hands on these, rest assured these will be reliable and accurate.

As far as other documents are concerned, you will need to do your research to find out which ones are genuine.

16. When was the puppy separated from the mother and fellow litter?
If the breeder quotes duration shorter than seven weeks, it is likely to have behavioural problems that will make handling more difficult. This is because the basic value exchange occurs while the puppy is still under the mother's care.
Early separation means the value exchange is incomplete. Such puppies are known to have personality issues that make handling difficult.

17. When will the puppy be ready for a ride home?
It is normal to keep the puppy intact with the mother for a minimum of seven weeks. Even after this period, some time will be needed to acclimatize it to foreign environments.
If the breeder seems to be in a hurry to get rid of the puppy, this is definitely the sign that raises suspicion!

18. How and when was the first Kangal couple imported?
As mentioned previously, this species is specific to Turkey. Anyone who says the breed is locally promoted definitely has no knowledge of the breed's origin.
Make sure the breeder can trace back the lineage to Turkey or you will end up settling for another breed in the name of Kangal dogs.

19. How are the puppies socialized?
Find out what was done to encourage puppies to socialize. The first lessons they learn usually come from their littermates.
If something else has been done (training etc) to promote socialization, make a mental note of it. This will definitely help you later on when you are trying to get the pet to adjust with your rules!

20. Has the puppy itself or anyone of its siblings been reported sick?
Keep in mind that the genetic code is similar for all littermates. A problem with one can almost certainly be expected with another. If the breeder is hesitant, feel free to ask for medical documents pertaining to other littermates.

21. How many visits to the veterinary doctor have been made?
Seek medical reports for each visit. Any discrepancy is supposed to be looked upon with distrust.

22. What does the puppy eat to meet its nutritional requirements?
Make a list of all the things it is known to tolerate well so you know what to feed it.
Some dogs/puppies may be accustomed to special meals. It is best to know this beforehand so you can conduct the preliminary shopping according to its wishes.

23. Describe a typical day in the life of the puppy.
It will give you sufficient insight about the activity level and demands of the pet.
Inquire about the shady areas to fully understand your puppy's needs. You definitely do not want surprises waiting for you at the other end!

24. What should I do to take care of it as the owner?
Inquire if you will be given continued assistance even after the contract has been signed.
A responsible breeder will be more concerned about the puppy's health rather than money and will therefore be available whenever you face any problems.
If s/he isn't, it is most probably because they are not well aware of the breed!

25. What are the best training methods to be used for this breed?
A person who has devoted a significant amount of time to

handling the specific breed will know the answer.
If the breeder is being too ambiguous or vague, it points towards inexperience and lack of knowledge.

26. How often will the puppy need to be groomed?
Again, the experienced breeder will be in a better state to give you an appropriate answer to this.
Hope to hear about its shedding season, its general messiness owing to its lifestyle and other similar facts.
"Daily" or "Weekly" is not really the answer you are looking for at this point!

27. How large will the puppy get?
Kangal dogs grow into huge animals. If the breeder cannot say so, s/he is most probably new to the breed.
It goes without saying that the breeder in this case is not the one you should be looking for!

28. Does the specific breed get along well with other animals?
This might be handy if you already have or plan to adopt more pets.
Kangal dogs, generally, do not welcome competition nicely. If the breeder fails to give this fact adequate emphasis, it is most probably because s/he is trying to get rid of the dogs. It should spark concern for your personal safety.

29. Can it be left alone?
There is no single word answer to this question.
Specifically about the Kangal breed, the breeder should deliberate about the energy reserve, the exercise requirement and the subsequent time span it can be left alone.
If the breeder is hesitant about sharing this information, there is definitely something wrong with the puppy in question.

30. Has the puppy been micro-chipped or tattooed?
It will simply be good to know about it beforehand. It is not a

prerequisite.
Micro chipping, however, might make it easier for you to locate your pet if it decides to take off into the wild in any direction!

If there are any other concerns or questions in your mind, feel free to inquire about them. Adopting a pet or living with one is not easy. You definitely want to be absolutely sure about your choices before you make them.

Your search for a responsible, genuine and reputable breeder does not end when you have received proper answers to these questions. The good ones want their puppies to go into good homes where they can settle down with ease.

So while you inquire about the breeder's authenticity, be prepared to be questioned in return so the breeder knows how serious you are about petting the Kangal dog. The next section covers this part in adequate detail.

b. Questions To Expect From the Breeder

The breeders will also want to ensure you are the right owner for the puppy available for adoption. So you should anticipate the breeder asking the following questions!

If s/he doesn't, the odds are high that the business is solely being run for profit and the breeder has no regard for the family or the well being of the puppy whatsoever. Naturally, this means trouble, as the money-minded breeder will seldom take responsibility for things that do not work out.

This also means that they will have no regard for the puppy's well being either on their own site or in the adopter's home. Amidst the rising number of frauds and reckless behaviour, you can play your role by at least selecting the breeder responsibly!

Here is what they should ask you:

1. What kind of a lifestyle do you have – laid back, athletic or somewhere in the middle?
It is important to match the personality of the dog with the personality of the owner for a problem-free association. A mismatch in this regard can result in serious disasters for both.
It is not unnatural for the breeder to be interested in your day-to-day activities. If your activity level is not adequately matched with the energetic nature of the Kangal dog, the breeder should be able to warn you beforehand!

2. Any prior experiences with dogs/puppies?
Experience works both ways.
An experienced breeder can help you make intelligent dog choices.
An experienced owner, such as you, can help the puppy feel at home and transit seamlessly from the breeder's space to the new abode.
After all, it is the puppy that is at the centre of the equation.

3. Are there any small children or other animals involved in the scenario?
They do impact the way the new addition to the family will react or adjust to the environment.
New pets around very small children are not encouraged for obvious reasons. So if there are any small children that your new acquisition is required to settle in with, an untrained Kangal dog might not be the best choice.

4. Where do you live?
The Kangal breed in particular is not meant for apartment life. You at least need a backyard – some open space – where it can exercise its control.
Likewise, different breeds have their own specifications. The responsible breeder will want to match up the dog's requirement with the resources available to make sure the puppy's care is not compromised.

It is best not to feign answers just to get the Kangal puppy – for all you know you might have to put it out at a later date because the canine fails to behave properly.

5. Are there fences or safety features installed in the house?
The Kangal dog has a tendency to chase anything it sees as a threat – whether it is humans or fly away objects like leaves or other animals. The fence definitely needs to be there before bringing in the pet.
If, by any chance, the fence is not in place as yet, the breeder will be interested to know by when it would be possible to get the safety measures installed – for the Kangal dog's benefit.

6. What is the purpose of the adoption?
The breeder will want to know if s/he is dealing with competition or with the final consumer.
If your adoption motives include raising a family dog, the breeder might mandate you to neuter or spay the animal (covered later) for its own health.
In other cases, the dealing will be substantially different.
In either case, don't hesitate to share your motives. For all you know you might end up with sterilized pairs of Kangal dogs, which will be of no use when it comes to breeding and procreation!

7. What do you know about this breed?
The breeder wants to know if you are up for the challenges faced while bringing up the Kangal breed. S/he would test your knowledge just to be sure you are aware about it.
Make sure you have done your research well or at least have some witty answers prepared to compel the breeder to talk.
If you come off as someone purchasing the Kangal dog for no good reason, it might make him or her rethink his or her decisions.

8. Are you aware of the costs?
Most first timers will not have any idea. Let the breeder educate you about the costs involved with maintaining a pet.
Apart from the substantial chunk that goes into its medical bills, the daily expenditure is also not child's play. Be mentally prepared for it all.
A general estimate for the upkeep of a Kangal dog is given later on in this book. Go through that to get an idea how the finances work.

The bottom line is that a responsible breeder wants the puppy to go into a good home and you would like a companion you can settle easily with. Lies will only make matters worse – for all participants.

It is best to be honest in this exchange for the benefit of all three parties involved – the breeder, the new owner and the poor little fellow whose fate is being decided!

It needs to be peaceful for all three parties involved to maximize the returns multifold.

9) Where to Buy and For How Much?

So you have a fair idea about how the Kangal dogs are, what to expect of them and how to search for a genuine breeder. What is the next step? Well, it is time to make the purchase – finally!

Keep in mind that the Kangal dogs are native to Turkey – so naturally this is the place where you can expect to find the purebreds. The recognition and popularity of this breed is more or less recent, so you can expect very few genuine Kangal breeders in your vicinity.

Getting the Kangal dog imported from Turkey may be the most logical solution; however, it is equally impractical and expensive as well. It is always better to have hands on experience seeing and feeling the dog before taking it home – just in case your expectations are wrecked.

Moreover, when it is about beyond borders, the exchange and return policy does not work as easily as you expect it to. You surely don't want to be stuck with an animal that fails to understand your orders and is powerful enough to knock down the entire house! Believe it; the Kangal dog has that kind of strength that you wouldn't want near your prized possessions!

The next best alternative is to look for a local Kangal breeder. You can come across quite a few if you research thoroughly and properly. Here are a few tips and tricks to help you make an intelligent purchase.

a. Establishing a Genuine Breeder

By hook or by crook, this is the first step you need to overcome so you know where to buy!

The last section covers in ample detail how you can establish if the breeder is genuine and authentic. The key is to ask all questions that come to your mind – even if it irritates the dealer. If the breeder is genuine enough, you can expect an equivalent number of questions and concerns from the other end.

Take your time in identifying the breeder – do not feel time bound!

Although you would love to have your pet shift in with you at the earliest possible, it is always better to check and recheck your options before settling for one – even if it takes months at stretch.

Never underestimate the importance and significance of references!

Be a part of a positive change that will help brighten the future of the Kangal breed!

b. Kangal Dogs in US

In the United States, you will be able to find a handful of fine Kangal breeders. However, the biggest problem you will face will be while determining if the breed is genuinely Kangal or not.

In the United States, the Kangal breed has not been recognized as a separate one – it is often considered the same as Anatolian Shepherd. Consequently, you are likely to come across quite a few Anatolian Shepherds in your search. Moreover, you need to be fully aware of what you are looking for in order to mark the difference.

In the United States, the AKC does not recognize the Kangal; the UKC (United Kennel Club) and the KDCA (Kangal Dog Club of America) does. It will be therefore be a good idea to seek these clubs for resources and references.

If you are looking to rescue some Kangal dogs, these clubs will have the most valuable resources for you.

On this note, try not to settle for online breeders. Firstly, you never know who is on the other end and you will never be able to figure it out until the scam has already engulfed you. This is especially true if you are not allowed to see or touch the specimen before making the payment.

Moreover, there are no pointers to substantiate whether the business is genuine or not. Generally, the authentic breeders do not try to establish any online presence. So instead of wasting time online, try looking for businesses with valid physical addresses that offer precisely the things you are looking for!

As far as the prices are concerned, rest assured the Kangal species are not cheap. There are two major reasons for this; firstly, it is a non-native breed and hence has import charges embedded in their cost at some point; secondly, there are very few genuine breeders so they are naturally inclined to charge a little extra for their unique offering!

You can expect a 4-6 month old Kangal bred locally to cost you $500 / £290 onwards. If you choose to have it shipped, be prepared to pay almost the equivalent amount in shipment charges as well – usually starting at $1,200/ £700 for the whole transaction. The prices can go up to several thousand dollars! Important Note: do NOT recommend you to buy a dog that is being "shipped" to you. It can't be a nice experience for the dog. However, with websites selling dogs popping up every where, sadly enough sometimes sellers do ship their dogs/ puppies. I recommend that you and pick up your dog from where-ever you bought it from.

And this is the one-time acquisition cost – it does not include the regular costs that will be incurred by your pet in the form of pet food, healthcare, medical insurance, toys, recreational activities, and so on and so forth!

The Kangal breed cannot be considered cheap from any perspective. In fact, some of the breeders would like to start their prices from a couple of thousand dollars to make up for the uniqueness of this breed. Evaluate your alternatives carefully in order to land yourself the best deal. The Kangal dog is a fine companion to have. It readily grows on you and your family. Its protective nature is what won it the title of Guardian Dog! It is up to you how much you are willing to sacrifice to let the association begin!

c. Kangal Dogs in the UK

If you are living in the UK, it definitely does not make sense to ask the breeder to show you the AKC papers. The Kennel Club of the UK is what leads the show in this part of the world.

As previously stated, the most natural and logical instinct to ensure a purebred is to get it shipped from its native homeland in Turkey. It is similarly impractical and expensive. The local breeders can help you overcome this problem easily provided you know what you are searching for and where you need to look!

The good thing about buying Kangal dogs in the UK is that the Kennel Club of the UK recently recognized and appreciated this breed. It now enjoys the status of a breed distinct from the Anatolian Shepherd. So it is relatively easier to establish the breed of the dog you are planning to purchase compared to the United States.

However, as in the United States, the breed is quite expensive due to its scarcity and uniqueness. Be prepared to invest in quite a few pounds to get the best Kangal dog on the block!

The starting price for Kangal puppies begins at £800 / $1300 and goes on to several thousands.

Don't forget to compute your regular maintenance cost and add it to the first month – you need to have your act together before bringing the new member of the family home.

You can ask for the Kennel Club of the UK papers to identify whether your choice is a champion breed. The Kennel Club of the UK registers not only the purebreds but also the crossbreeds. Hence they have the most extensive database of dogs you can imagine!

Online Kangal dog sellers are not a very good option for obvious reasons. If you are new to this, try asking around your neighbourhood to see where they get their canine companions.

A person already in possession of a Kangal dog is the best person to seek this information from. However, other breed owners might also be in a possibly competitive state to guide you through the acquisition process.

10) Getting Registered

In different parts of the world, it is ordained by law to get your dog registered with the relevant authorities. This is one way of ensuring that the canine is well kept, adequately vaccinated, and/or micro chipped.

In some states, one-time registration is required whereas in some others the registration (or more commonly known as the license) will need to be renewed on a yearly basis. It keeps the state records updated as per the progress of the Kangal dog.

There are infinite benefits of getting your dog registered.

Firstly and most importantly, it keeps you safe from unnecessary penalties as a result of breaking the rules. The charges put forth against you in case you are caught with an unregistered dog can be as drastic as $250 / £145 at a time. It is considerably better and smart to invest in a $10 - $20 / £5 to £10 license instead.

Moreover, in case your Kangal companion decides to take a walk and fails to find its way back home, the license increases the chances of getting it back by a considerable degree. Not only does it make the Kangal dog uniquely identifiable but also helps the rescuers in locating you!

On this note, it is worth mentioning that in several parts of the world, many dogs are euthanized. Most of the brutality is associated with the dog being unregistered or "stray".

While some rescue organizations might be able to get in their say, most of the times this luck does not work out for them. Getting your dogs registered prevents your canine friend against this unfortunate luck and helps you in getting back your lost pal!

However, most importantly, registration (at dog clubs) is important to preserve the sanctity of the dog gene pool. Registration marks your pet as a pedigree – especially if you are successful in attaining the AKC papers.

The authorities that evaluate the dog have extremely strict rules and guidelines. Every aspect of the canine has to be perfect in order to receive the registration papers.

Moreover, as in the case of AKC, the names and presence of parents also needs to be registered. The process of registration (at the dog clubs) is robust, stringent and extremely intricate. This helps establish the authentic purebreds.

In the case of the Kennel Club of the UK, owners are allowed to register crossbreeds as well. Nevertheless, once your pet is registered it can then take part in a number of socialization events held each year by these clubs. It automatically becomes more valuable in case you decide to transfer ownership to someone else in the near future.

Registration – especially at reputable and well-known organizations like the AKC – is what determines whether the dog you have purchased or are about to purchase is a purebred or not. If the breeder fails to cooperate in helping you register the species, rest assured they lack authenticity. It is also a way to establish whether the breeder is genuine or not.

The benefits of getting your pet registered are in abundance; so what are you still thinking about? Get your canine registered at the earliest and you can prevent yourself from major heartbreaks later on!

11) Preparing Yourself

If you have shortlisted the breeder, made your choice of puppy and are almost halfway through with the payment and ownership transfer, half of your work is done! The arrival of the new companion is but a matter of days!

While this is undoubtedly an exhilarating experience, think again – have you prepared adequately to accommodate your new friend? There are a lot of things that need to be done well before you make the move. Make sure you have answered questions like "Where will your pet sleep? What will it eat? How will you keep it occupied?" and so on and so forth! If you haven't, it is high time you start planning for all these concerns before they hit you head on in the near future. Keep in mind that these chores cannot be left until after the dog comes to your home. With the bubbly pet taking up most of your time, you will not have any time to go out shopping!

Furthermore, it is highly unlikely that you will be able to go out shopping within two weeks of purchase – the new pet will prove to be quite a handful!

Have your act together before it puts you at any sort of disadvantage. The next few pages aim to walk you through the basic necessities you need to fulfil in order to assist your pet through its initial transitional phase.

a. Preliminary Shopping List

Be fully prepared to receive your pet in a travel crate – this will be arranged by most breeders. As the pet is new and possibly bewildered, it is best not to carry it in your arms.

In addition to this vital necessity (to make transportation possible), there are a dozen other things you will need to purchase so that your pet can survive a minimum of two weeks.

If you are planning to take your new pet shopping even before it has settled, rest assured it is a sure recipe for disaster. Have enough stocks to last you two weeks. By this time, your pet will have adjusted to the new owner, new rules and new lifestyle. Hence it will pose fewer challenges while handling.

Here is a list of things you need to purchase – before the new one walks in!

1. Visit to the vet.
It is like a gift from you to your dog – something that it will definitely be thankful for even if it is not able to say it out loud. Have it vaccinated for all major diseases and draft up a schedule for regular checkups. Mark it on your calendar so you don't miss out on it.
Remember, your vet can see beyond the furry, shiny coat and hence is in a better state to identify any imminent health problems and diseases.
As in the case of the breeder, take your time in locating a certified and genuine veterinary doctor.

2. Pet Food! This includes food, treats and all other form of edibles for your pet.
This is one thing you will need within 24 hours of getting the dog home. Moreover, this is one thing that is directly related to its health, rationality, irritability and resistance.

Try to get the same stocks of pet food your canine is already accustomed to at the breeder's – so it can feel at home. Be foresighted and get enough food to last you a minimum of two weeks.

3. Food and Water bowls. As much as you would like it, your canine friends cannot feast with you using your kitchen utensils. They need to have their own bowls for food and water.
Make sure you have purchased these beforehand to minimize the stress of finding an alternative impromptu when the need arises.
Also keep in mind that your pet associates these bowls with nutrition and will continue to do so for a long time. So it is a good idea to invest in high-quality and durable bowls.
Have a good look at the breeder's options before making your decision so that your new friend does not feel like a stranger.

4. ID tags, collars and leash. These accessories mark your pet dog and establish your ownership for the world to see.
It is also imperative for you to get these affairs in order well before you get your new companion home. Feeling as a captive being taken away from home, your new pet is likely to make a dash into the unknown whenever it is given the opportunity.
In a foreign neighbourhood, the chances of it finding its way to your home are next to impossible. So make sure your new friend is fastened adequately to prevent such unfortunate incidences.
Even if it does, the identification documents around its neck will prove to be a lifesaver – someone else who comes across your dog will be able to return it home if your dog carries its home address!
Keep the Kangal dog's size, strength and personality traits in mind while shopping for its identification accessories.

5. Dog bed. After a long day of getting accustomed to foreign practices and obeying orders from a relatively unknown master, your dog needs adequate rest so that it wakes up fresh and healthy the next morning.

A dog bed lined with soft linens and soft cushions work well. If your pet does not sleep well, it will eventually lead it towards bigger health problems.
So make sure you place its bed in a secluded and silent corner of the house. Also, help your pet associate this space with "night" and "sleep" so it is easier to command it to rest.
Rest assured, this is not something you can leave for later – your canine friend needs a good night's sleep every night!
On this note, keep in mind that the regular size of a Kangal dog is much larger than most other breeds. So shop for its bed accordingly.
Purchasing a size or two bigger will be a good idea as the Kangal breed has a knack of growing up faster than most other breeds.

6. Dog toys. Dogs don't sleep well with a whole lot of built up energy in their bodies. Assuming you don't have the time or the will to walk your pet every evening/morning in the first few days of association, dog toys are the second best alternative to achieve this motive.
It helps in keeping your pet occupied and entertained (without your active effort). Moreover, dog toys are also an effective way of stimulating the dog's brain and helping it develop its capacities.
Use intelligent dog toys and obstacles to help your canine friend develop intellectually and physically – as it would if it were to live in the wild!

7. Travel crate. You won't need it immediately (unless your breeder fails to offer the initial carry crate) but you eventually will.
Imagine the first time you go out shopping after your new pet makes it home. How do you imagine you will carry the fragile being? Carrying it in your arms, though an impressive gesture, will not work well as your pet will feel threatened by the sudden presence of hundreds of other shoppers.
On top of this, there are other places you might need to go to –

office, veterinary doctor, your own doctor and others – that will definitely not accommodate an open dog. So it is better to purchase a travel crate well beforehand to keep away from embarrassments.
Also keep in mind that your Kangal dog is not like other dogs, so you will probably need to buy a much bigger and sturdier travel crate.

8. Dog clothes. This becomes exceptionally imperative if you are planning on purchasing your Kangal companion during the winter.
Do remember to buy a few warm clothes for your dog if you plan on keeping it outdoors – even in the summer. The cold can get to its skin and make it ill before you would realize what has happened.
Keep your defences up to protect your pet against all odds. Although the Kangal dog is likely to have a heavier coat to battle the winter chill, it nevertheless pays to play your role as the owner.
For the Kangal breed, make sure you buy a size that is "XXL". Even if it is too loose in the beginning, it will readily fit well.

9. Grooming supplies. Dogs are inquisitive creatures. They have inexplicable interest in finding out what is hidden in the darkest of corners. They can easily be led to places by the smallest of insects. So naturally, they don't last a week without getting dirty. Having grooming supplies beforehand therefore is a good idea. Imagine having to go to the supermarket with an unkempt dog that clearly says its master does not care!
Be foresighted enough to prepare for things that are expected to happen. Make sure you search through all alternatives on the market before settling for a few – it helps you get the best possible items!
Make sure you have ample supplies to last two weeks. It would typically include shampoo, scrub, dental hygiene solutions, nail clippers, hair tonic, conditioners, and everything else that you

would like to use for your new pet's beauty. The sky is the limit. Even so, it is recommended not to use a lot of chemicals on your pet, as an excess of everything is detrimental.

10. Puppy pads. No one likes to witness a trail of unsightly liquids or solids winded all across the house. The odour makes it even more unbearable. Do yourself a favour and use puppy pads for the first few days – especially if your canine friend is not yet potty trained.
Train it to use the outdoors for relieving itself. It will become possible and tolerable over-time!

Once you are out on the shopping spree, you will come across a number of other items that are not on this list but might apparently look useful. Evaluate its utility in the light of your pet before making your purchase.

However, if it seems like an absolute necessity, it is better not to let it be left for a later date.

Admittedly, these accessories summed up with the cost of acquiring a pet (payment to the breeder, registrations etc) can amount to a significant portion of your savings. So you need to be mentally prepared for this kind of expenditure.

It is expected to be an association of a decade or two, so rest assured it will be an ongoing expense rather than just a one-time incident!

Keep in mind that most of the items on your shopping list will last quite a few years before they become unusable, broken or "too small" for use (provided you make intelligent decisions in the first place!).

Having a new companion inevitably calls for a few adjustments. You will need to make quite a few sacrifices to let your new friend settle in. It will be worth the time and effort!

b. Proofing Your House

Talking about adjustments, there are quite a few alterations you will need to make to your house to make it fit for your Kangal dog. It is all in your best interests and for your pet's well being.

Puppies, especially those that are teething, like nibbling at things they do not realize might be of importance to you – for instance, your sofa, your chairs, curtains and other accessories around the house.

They also like flexing their claws at things that are resistant like wooden doors.

Here is what you need to do to keep your property and puppy safe from damages.

1. A tall fence around your home.
In fact, the breeder who is offering you a Kangal puppy is likely to inquire about your home before handing over the beloved puppy.
This is because Kangal dogs have an aptitude of following stray animals and strange noises out into the wild. Given their magnanimous size, you need really tall fences to contain them within the boundaries of your house.
Putting tall fences around your home makes it Kangal-proof. It is best to get these installed before you bring the puppy/dog home.
Also make sure the area under the fence has also been proofed.
The Kangal dog is known for its digging habits.
Beware of suspicious dirt piles and unnecessarily dirty paws – your pet might be up to something.

2. Install safety latches in every possible place.
This includes all cabinets and cupboards in the kitchen and elsewhere in the house that are used to stock toxic chemicals like cleaners etc.

You definitely don't want your Kangal dog to discover these or try experimenting with them.
It is also a good idea to install devices on the doors that enable them to close on their own. Keep nurseries, personal rooms and other similar places out of reach of your canine.
If your pet chokes on your child's toy or some other product of similar nature, rest assured the results are not likely to be pleasant.
Keep all medicines, chemicals, cleaners and other potentially hazardous solutions stored behind locked doors at all times!

3. Safe wirings.
Under normal circumstances, leaving a wire or two lying haphazard on the ground is not a big problem; but this is not the case once you have a pet dog in the house.
Inquisitive as they are, they are likely to try playing with the unsheathed wire using their claws. During this little adventure, they might end up exposing the internal copper wirings, which may lead to an electric shock.
It is therefore infinitely better to keep these wires stowed away from plain view in the corners of the room.
Also use a protective covering made from durable plastic to prevent scratches.
Give your pet other safe objects to play with so the wires do not catch its attention!

4. Keep small, potentially dangerous and fragile items away from your pet's reach.
This includes all kinds of decoration pieces made from crystal, glass or other similar material that shatters on impact.
All CDs, DVDs, keys, remotes, kitchen utensils, containers, sharp-edged items, plastic bags and other similar objects that have the tendency to become lethal should be stocked behind locked doors.
Your Kangal pet does not have as much sense to realize when it is

headed for some major trouble. Care for it as you would if it were your offspring!

5. Pet door.
You will need to install one in your main door to allow your dog to move in and out of the house as it pleases.
Make sure it is the right size and does not strangle the canine. Also make sure there are no obstructions to its course.
Alternatively, be prepared to see some claw marks on the door if your canine friend finds it closed when and if it needs to go outdoors. This also curtails the call of nature, which might be quite messy to clean up.
Invest in a worthwhile pet door to make things easier.

6. The bathroom needs dog-proofing as well.
Keep the door closed at all times – use an automatic door lock if necessary.
The flush bowl is an exceptionally attractive place for your pet and it is equally hazardous too. And this does not even cover the dangers of slippery floors!
Best to keep the door of your bathroom locked to ban your pet's entry into it.

7. Dog-foe plants, edibles and objects to be stored away from reach.
Surprisingly, most dogs don't tolerate chocolates well. So don't leave your wrappers lying around.
If you have any plants that your pet is allergic to, you need to make arrangements to discourage contact. Either change the position of the plant or put it in a place where your pet is not allowed.

8. Use barriers where needed.
This applies equally to indoor uses as well as outdoor uses.
You might want to proof your sofas and cabinets by using a barrier/grill.

If you have an outdoor garden, don't ever leave your dog unattended until and unless you are looking for a major makeover!
Use barriers in front of pools and every other object you don't want your pet to sniff around. It is for its own good!

9. Be careful while using detergents, cleaners and other chemicals.
Their remains are still dangerous for your pet.
The garage should be free from chemicals if it is a "can-visit" area for your pet.
Keep your car in regular check to prevent leakages and spills.

Try your best to keep your pet under supervision at all times. This way you get to control small and innocent mistakes from becoming life-threatening situations.

Once you are satisfied with your proofing efforts, try looking at the situation from your puppy's point of view.

Crouch down on all fours and look around your place from the eye level of a puppy.

You can turn this into a creative activity for the little ones in your house. Identify all possible hazards and threats and fix them as soon as possible. It is best if your puppy does not have the liberty to explore the hazards before you!

The first few days/weeks are extremely crucial for your pet to settle down. If you successfully make it through these tough days, rest assured there is a rainbow at the other end!

It is always better to be safe than sorry. However, in case an accident has taken place or you suspect something is seriously wrong with your pet – probably because it has started acting very weird lately – don't waste a minute and rush it to a vet.

A problem nipped in the bud is much better than a situation that needs to be controlled once it has already reached beyond your control! The rest should be fine!

Chapter 4: Getting Used To Your Dog

You now have a fair idea about what you should expect from your association with a Kangal dog.

If you have the kind of energy and resources needed to build a relationship with Kangal dog, then go for it!

If not, it is better to leave the thought altogether rather than to leave your canine friend stranded in the middle of nowhere after spending some time with it.

Here is what you should expect to see once you're done with the preliminaries and are about to bring it home. The first few days are always the toughest. The going gets easier from then on.

1) The Adjustment

It is highly unlikely for the new puppy to come into your home and feel like a member all of a sudden. Likewise, to expect a new puppy to know and abide by all your rules is equally farfetched. You need to give your new friend time and space to blend into the foreign environment.

While your new companion adjusts, make sure you give it no reason to believe it is superior to its masters. Make sure you never let it take the lead. Such gestures will aggravate into a major problem later on.

Always walk ahead of the Kangal dog to administer your superiority. If you let the dog lead you or any of your family members even once, it will begin considering humans as flock. The rest can become quite distressing as the Kangal refuses to follow orders and degenerates into a major menace rapidly.

Also use disciplinary actions wherever needed to rectify your pet's behaviour. Keep in mind that such "strictness" or "brutality" (as some people might call it) is imperative and is only likely to work if used in the first few days. If not, you will end up reinforcing its notoriety.

If you are planning on changing its diet for any reason (possibly because the dog food it was provided with at the breeders is not readily available in your vicinity), you need to do so slowly. If you change its food all of a sudden, it will quit eating altogether.

For the first day, resort to the "old" dog food it is accustomed to. This helps build credibility and a relationship of trust. The next day you can introduce the new diet but make sure at least 75% of its total consumption is based on the old food.

On the third day, you can offer your pet 50% of the old food and 50% of the new one. Observe its reactions closely. In case any adverse reactions become evident, you might want to stay put with the old dog food. Search for online sellers if acquiring the particular dog food in your vicinity is difficult.

On the fourth day, you can reduce the quantity of old dog food down to 25%. You would have successfully transited your pet to its new diet. Hopefully by this time if you start offering it the new dog food, withdrawal symptoms will be negligible.

If there are any other changes you are hoping to make, do so gradually over time. Your pet will not absorb any abrupt changes positively. In fact, it may give rise to behavioural problems due to an exaggerated sense of being away from home.

Train your pet to obey your orders and use any means possible to achieve this. Training sessions are a good place to acclimatize your Kangal dog with the new code of conduct it is required to follow. You should train your pet across a wide range of skills and activities. This does not only include simple actions like "sit", "stand" and "fetch" but also those that pertain to others' safety.

Take some time to indulge in activities that help in building trust. During the first few days, it is normal for your pet to remain aloof from the family members and avoid encounters with them. At times, the new ones might feel compelled to make a dash out of the open doors in order to attain their freedom.

Keep adequate safety measures intact to prevent the Kangal from escaping your premises. At the same time, indulge in activities that help build a bond between you and your newfound pet. Once your pet is over with the initial hesitation, it will pave the way for a healthy relationship.

Your pet can take up to two weeks to fully administer your ownership. This is the most crucial period so you need to be intelligent with your decisions. Keep it under constant supervision and train it in matters concerning well being – for your own good as well as for your pet.

Whatever you do, you need to maintain your patience with the feeble canine at all times. If you shout at it or hurt it in any way, it will instil a sense of fear in the pet. This will hamper the development of a worthwhile relationship.

There are a lot of things you will need to teach your pet. Even with the initial value exchange at the breeder's place, a great many things need to be taught. One of the most notorious is potty training.

While doing so, maintain your patience and learn to forgive your canine's mistakes. A detailed guide on how to go about the potty training phase is given later in this book. Consult it for a viable plan of action to meet the desired ends.

It is not a matter of minutes or seconds but a couple of years. So it is better to lay sound foundations to build a positive relationship on.

2) Sharing Space with Other Animals

The Kangal is an over-protective breed. So naturally you can expect it not to respond well to competition. However, if you already have other animals in the house that you would like to introduce to your pet, make sure this meeting does not go unsupervised.

If your Kangal dog assumes its defensive mode at the sight of the new companion, try to subdue it with words of comfort. All the while, maintain a steady hold at its leash. Consider the emotions of the other pet as well as this one – how would the other one like it if the Kangal dog was to get within range and bite it?

This kind of socialization is best left for a time after the Kangal dog has been through the preliminary training phases. This way, you can ensure that your Kangal dog will at least respond to your orders. If you try rushing through this phase, you might end up putting your other pet's life in peril.

If you are planning on bringing in a few more pets along with the Kangal, make sure you give it ample time to settle down before introducing it to other animals. You want the meeting to be successful and largely uneventful – so it is best not to hurry.

Kangal dogs find it easier to socialize with humans compared to animals. However, if other pets are of a subdued nature – opposite to the Kangal dog's leading nature – your canine companion is likely to consider it as its flock and hence guard it. The most evident example of this association is the fact that the Kangal breed has historically been used to guard livestock in different parts of Turkey. Beware of bringing in dominant personality pets though – Kangal dogs and such pets will most probably not blend in well.

Over time, however, most associations work out well – even those that apparently appear impossible. It'll need patience and perseverance on your behalf to get things working in your favour.

You will need to assure and reassure all your pets that you are equally available for all and that everyone is supposed to live in peace and harmony rather than see each other as competition. Once you become successful in getting this message across in the right way, it will become easier for you to manage several different pets at a time.

3) Growth and Development – What to Expect?

The Kangal dog usually has a lifespan of 12 to 15 years – more if you take good care of your canine friend! It is considered as one of the larger dog breeds and is expected to reach impressive heights.

What is more, the Kangal puppies grow quickly – about twice in size compared to their age. So it is always a good idea to buy dog accessories a size or two bigger so that it can at least serve a year of useful life.

The Kangal dog continues to grow for the first three years of its life. You will witness consistent physical changes in your pet for at least three years, after which you can consider the Kangal dog to have matured. Usually, physical changes include the changes in height, weight, physical features and others.

The Kangal dogs are massive; they can rise up to six feet high while standing on their hind legs. Naturally, they need a lot of space to live.

So if you are accustomed to the small apartment life or if you are thinking of purchasing a Kangal to accompany you in your flat, such an arrangement will most probably not work. The plan will backfire as soon as you realize how quickly the puppy seems to be growing.

With their massive size, their humungous weight is also more or less justified. Comparatively, though, they will be lighter than most other large dog breeds.

If truth be told, at some point in time, you can expect to see a large and heavy dog relaxing on your sofa that follows your orders but is otherwise invincible.

On this note, there is another important characteristic of your Kangal dog that is worthy of a mention. Keep in mind that the Kangal dog gets bored easily. So you will need to unleash your true creativity in developing activities for it. Not only should the activities aim to tire the Kangal dog out but also stimulate its mind for a strategic, problem solving thought process.

In addition, when it comes to strategic problem solving techniques, keep in mind that the Kangal breed is an intelligent one. It can learn basic tasks like opening the front door and untying a knot simply by observation. The best thing to do is to prevent the Kangal from observing the tasks that you would not want it to repeat later on.

You might need to come up with a new plan of action very frequently. Be prepared to invest a lot of time and effort in building activities for your Kangal dog. It will help you groom the canine into a fine companion.

4) Ways to Bond with Your Kangal Dog

Building a bond takes time and there is no doubt about it. It is the same way with every other living being – be it an animal or even a fellow human being.

If you have some quality time to spend with your Kangal dog, it will be the beginning of a lasting relationship.

Indulge in activities that make your dog feel loved. For instance, build obstacle courses for your dog. Treat your pet with something whenever it overcomes a hurdle and encourage it to keep moving on.

The traditional “fetch” game is quite some exercise for your canine friend and it even leaves a lot less on your plate to look after. However, do remember to improvise on the game rules from time to time to keep the Kangal dog's interest in tact.

Let it cuddle around your legs and hug it often. Your attention is what your pet recognizes as love. If nothing else, you need to take time out to provide this comfort for your pet.

For the Kangal breed in particular, the importance of exercise cannot be undermined. It is easily the best way to bond with your canine companion. Take it out for long walks of varying intensity and your Kangal will remain fit, healthy and happy.

Make sure you spend adequate time with your Kangal dog and indulge in activities that stimulate and tire it – it works to promote its development as well as the bond.

Kangal dogs love surprises so you need to innovate frequently. Build different obstacle courses as soon as you realize your pet has learnt its way through the current one. Indulge in different activities to keep it involved.

If you are careful about its needs, it will automatically reciprocate your emotions. It is simple and easy – so don't complicate it for yourself or for your pet.

Treat it as a member of the family and let it be that way. In any case, Kangal dogs have a protective nature. So it is better to remain on their better side.

The Kangal dog is not supposed to be used for fighting activities. Although it is fully equipped with the strength and valour to indulge in fighting other dogs, such practices are strictly inhibited for numerous reasons.

Firstly, it undermines the importance of the Kangal breed as a family dog. Just as you would not want other pet dogs to get into fights and/or get hurt, you should not put the Kangal dog in a difficult situation. It is a Guardian dog, not a fighting one.

Moreover, this also means you are instilling the wrong kind of values in your pet. It will try to be the leader of the pack and may therefore get involved in all kinds of fights just to establish its supremacy over the other.

It will continue to fight and rebel within the ring as well as outside. Eventually, this may lead to the Kangal dog straying away from being a dependable family dog. What was then the whole point of getting and training a Kangal dog to fight that fails to obey you?

If you want what is best for your Kangal dog, take the time to make an effort towards it. Understand its needs and try to fulfil them. You wouldn’t find the Kangal dog being ungrateful about the things you do for it.

5) The Good and the Bad about Kangal Dogs

The association works when there is an equal contribution from both counterparts. Regardless of whether you are purchasing a Kangal dog for the purpose of companionship or for guarding your livestock, there are certain aspects that you will need to adjust to.

Here is a little insight about the Kangal breed – what makes it desirable and what puts your decisions in doubt. Read through these carefully – they might help you differentiate between the “tolerable”, “adjustable” and the outright “intolerable” so you can make well-informed decisions about petting a Kangal dog.

a. The Good Part

Kangal dogs are a livestock guardian breed by nature. Here is what you can consider to be appreciable about them. These characteristics make the Kangal breed desirable as a family dog:

1. Nurturing behaviour.
Whatever they come to consider as their flock receives the utmost care. They help livestock animals grow under their protection. It is a built-in emotion that the Kangal dog possesses for those animals with not-so-strong personalities.

2. Ability to Fight off Threats.
The Kangal dog on its own is capable of fighting off wolves and other beasts in the wild. It will go to all extents in order to save its flock from all kinds of threats.
It is not an attacker by nature. It will initially try to ward off the threat by barking and howling.
If the predator does not take the hint, then attacking and defending is the Kangal dog's last resort. In most cases, the Kangal dog is likely to emerge victorious from the clash.

3. Good with children.
Most ferocious dogs don't blend in well with children. This is not the case with the Kangal breed.
These beings are absolutely gentle around kids and will consider them as their flock too.
However, the same cannot be said about kids they are not formally introduced with.
Any and every stranger will initially be considered as a threat until the owner takes time to formally introduce the newcomer. This will administer the fact that the "new" people are safe and hence not supposed to be attacked.

4. Ideal for rugged places.
The Kangal dog prefers living in the wild. Open fields and

pastures are therefore easily patrolled by them.
By looking at its history, it becomes evident that the breed is accustomed to executing its duties across rugged terrains.
Keeping it confined to small spaces is therefore not a very good idea.

5. Intelligent guardians.
If you assign two or more Kangal dogs with the responsibility of safeguarding livestock, they will divide the territory and then cover it.
Alternatively, they might take shifts to patrol the grounds and keep it covered at all times.
When working together, they know how to make the most of their association.
Moreover, it has been observed that Kangal dogs are generally more vigilant in the darkness of the night compared to broad daylight.
This further emphasizes its intelligence in determining the most vulnerable times and hence developing contingencies for it accordingly.

6. A "greener" and more effective solution to threats.
As mentioned previously, killing or attacking is not the Kangal dog's first instinct.
Moreover, they can ward off the threat of wild beasts in a better and more consistent manner compared to mechanical safety measures including lights and sirens – something the beasts get used to after some time.
In other words, they offer the peace of mind attached with the security of livestock without the fear of unnecessary bloodshed.

7. More active and vigilant at night.
It points towards the breed's intelligence. This leaves fewer worries on the hands of the owner.
The guardian dog will not only protect the livestock from danger but also round them off in pens if need be.

The owner can leave the property for brief periods with the Kangal in charge. More often, the owner will come back to witness perfect peace and harmony almost as good as the time s/he left it with.

8. An impressive lifespan.
Most large sized dogs don't survive over 6 years of age but the Kangal breed is slightly different.
With a lifespan ranging between 10 to 15 years, they make impressive and lasting companions and guardians.

9. Kangal dogs are more powerful than most large dog breeds.
Numerous Kangal owners have observed it across the world. They exhibit power and strength much more advanced than other large dog breeds.
So whether it is about the jaw strength, their pulling capability or any other demonstration of power, you can expect the Kangal dog to put up an impressive and entertaining rebellion against you!

What more could you possibly ask for?

b. The Bad Part

Everything is not as seamlessly perfect as it seems in the first impression. There are quite a few things about the Kangal breed, which will compel you to reconsider your decision.

Nevertheless, if you have time to spare to train the Kangal, it might lead you towards a better and brighter future.

Here are a few downsides pertaining to the Kangal breed that you need to be careful about.

They are no reasons why you should not consider a Kangal dog. It only implies to put you on your guard about the things that can affect your repute negatively.
1. Extremely strong willed creatures.

Training needs to begin during puppyhood to make them subservient.
At times, handling Kangal dogs will prove to be a major challenge. Their training technique also tends to be different as they can only be involved if they are intrigued – routine actions seldom attract their attention.
If you let their disobedience grow into a habit, be prepared to witness a Kangal that is simply uncontrollable!

2. High maintenance costs.
Due to its massive size, consequently, its diet and other regular necessities will be more or larger. So their maintenance costs, in general, are much higher than most other regular or small sized dogs.
If you don't have the kind of finances you need to provide for a Kangal dog's maintenance, it is better not to get into a commitment that you can obviously not fulfil.

3. Prone to health problems pertaining to environmental exposure.
As they prefer the outdoors, the likeness for them to fall prey to health complications is quite evident.
Fleas and heartworms are common – just to mention a few.
Accordingly, their medical costs are also slightly higher than most other dog breeds.
With proper pet insurance coverage, however, you can relieve quite some burden off your savings!

4. Night time barking.
This is one thing the Kangal dog is outright famous for and hence does not work well in neighbourhoods.
It will take extensive training and reassurances to keep the Kangal dog quiet at night.
Even the rustle of a leaf is reason enough for it to start barking in the middle of the night.
So you definitely need to be careful about this characteristic when employing it in friendly and inhabited neighbourhoods.

If there are empty stretches of land on either side of your residence, then this might not prove to be as much of a problem as in the previous case.

5. Active socialization efforts needed.
They are extremely aggressive animals, especially to those they consider as “foreign”.
So you will need to play an active role in helping them socialize with other people.
Although getting into trouble unnecessarily is not really common for the Kangal dog, it is not exactly unheard of either. So you need to train them to recognize threats, as you would see it.

6. A natural leader.
You need to show it its place from the beginning if you want to establish your ownership and supremacy over the dog.
Never let it lead you while walking or moving around. Once it establishes itself as a leader, it will be extremely challenging to subdue it. Make sure you’ve done your homework well.
On the same note, do not let the dog explore the lands unsupervised. The Kangal dogs have a habit of marking their territory where they rule. This will eventually lead to a conflict of interest and ownership!

Despite all this, the Kangal breed is undoubtedly a desirable one. People (and the dog) learn to adapt to one another with time. If you’ve survived the first few years, the remaining years are likely to be extremely rewarding. There are significantly higher chances you would be looking for another Kangal dog once the current tenure has expired.

Chapter 5: House Training

1) Human Training

House training, house breaking, or *"potty"* training, is a critical first step in the education of any new puppy, and the first part of a successful process is training the human guardian.

When you bring home your new Kangal puppy, they will be relying upon your guidance to teach them what they need to learn.

When you provide your puppy with your consistent patience and understanding, they are capable of learning rules at a very early age, and house training is no different, especially since it's all about establishing a regular routine.

Potty training a new puppy takes time and patience — how much time depends entirely upon you.

Check in with yourself and make sure your energy remains consistently calm and patient and that you exercise plenty of compassion and understanding while you help your new puppy learn their new bathroom rules.

Kangal puppies and dogs flourish with routines and so do humans, therefore, the first step is to establish a daily routine that will work well for both canine and human alike.

For instance, depending upon the age of your Kangal puppy, make a plan to take them out for a bathroom break every two hours and stick to it because while you are in the beginning stages of potty training, the more vigilant and consistent you can be, the quicker and more successful your results will be.

Generally speaking, while your puppy is still growing, a young puppy can hold it approximately one hour for every month of their age.

This means that if your 2-month-old puppy has been happily snoozing for a couple of hours, as soon as they wake up, they will need to go outside.

Some of the first indications or signs that your puppy needs to be taken outside to relieve themselves will be when you see them:

- Sniffing around
- Circling
- Looking for the door
- Whining, crying or barking
- Acting agitated

It will be important to always take your Kangal puppy out first thing every morning, and immediately after they wake up from a nap as well as soon after they have finished eating a meal or having a big drink of water.

Your happy praise goes a long way towards encouraging and reinforcing future success when your Kangal puppy makes the right decisions, so let them know you are happy when they do their business in the right place.

Initially, treats can be a good way to reinforce how pleased you are that your puppy is learning to go potty in the right place.

Slowly treats can be removed and replaced with your happy praise.

Next, now that you have a new puppy in your life, you will want to be flexible with respect to adapting your schedule to meet the requirements that will help to quickly teach your Kangal puppy their new bathroom routine.

This means not leaving your puppy alone for endless hours at a time because firstly, they are sensitive pack animals that need companionship and your direction at all times, plus long periods alone will result in the disruption of the potty training schedule you have worked hard to establish.

If you have no choice but to leave your puppy alone for many hours, make sure that you place them in a paper lined room or pen where they can relieve themselves without destroying your favourite carpet or new hardwood flooring.

Remember, your Kangal is a growing puppy with a bladder and bowels that they do not yet have complete control over and you will have a much happier time and better success if you simply train yourself to pay attention to when your young companion is showing signs of needing to relieve themselves.

2) Bell Training

A very easy way to introduce your new Kangal puppy to house training is to begin by teaching them how to ring a doorbell whenever they need to go outside.

Ringing a doorbell is not only a convenient alert system for both you and your Kangal puppy or dog, your visitors will be most impressed by how smart your dog is.

A further benefit of training your puppy to ring a bell is that you will not have to listen to your puppy or dog whining, barking or howling to be let out, and your door will not become scratched up by their nails.

Unless you prefer to purchase an already manufactured doggy doorbell or system, take a trip to your local novelty store and purchase a small bell that has a nice, loud ring.

Attach the bell to a piece of ribbon or string and hang it from a door handle or tape it to a doorsill near the door where you will be taking your puppy out when they need to relieve themselves. The string will need to be long enough so that your Kangal puppy can easily reach the bell with their nose or a paw.

Next, each time you take your puppy out to go potty, say the word *"Out"*, and use their paw or their nose to ring the bell. Praise them for this *"trick"* and immediately take them outside.

The only down side to teaching your Kangal puppy or dog to ring a bell when they want to go outside is that even if they don't actually have to go out to relieve themselves, but just want to go outside because they are bored, you will still have to take them out every time they ring the bell.

There are many types and styles of *"gotta' go"* commercially manufactured bells you could choose, ranging from the elegant **"Poochie Bells™"** that hang from a doorknob, the simple **"Tell Bell™"** that sits on the floor, or various high tech door chime systems that function much like a doggy intercom system where they push a pad with their paw and it rings a bell.

Whatever doorbell system you choose for your Kangal puppy, once they are trained, this type of an alert system is an easy way to eliminate accidents in the home.

3) Kennel Training

Kennel training is always a good idea for any puppy early in their education, because it can be utilized for many different situations, including keeping them safe while travelling inside a vehicle and being a very helpful tool for house training.

When purchasing a kennel for your Kangal puppy, always buy a kennel that will be the correct size for your puppy once they become an adult.
The kennel will be the correct size if an adult Kangal can stand up and easily turn around inside their kennel.

When you train your Kangal puppy to accept sleeping in their own kennel at night time, this will also help to accelerate their potty training, because no puppy or dog wants to relieve themselves where they sleep, which means that they will hold their bladder and bowels as long as they possibly can.

Always be kind and compassionate and remember that a puppy will be able to hold it approximately one hour for every month of their age.

Generally, a Kangal puppy that is three months old will be able to hold it for approximately three hours, unless they just ate a meal or had a big drink of water.

Be watchful and consistent so that you learn your puppy's body language, which will alert you to when it's time for them to go outside.

Presenting them with familiar scents, by taking them to the same spot in the yard or the same street corner, will help to remind and encourage them that they are outside to relieve themselves.

Use a voice cue to remind your puppy why they are outside, such as *"go pee"* and always remember to praise them every time they relieve themselves in the right place so that they quickly understand what you expect of them and will learn to *"go"* on cue.

4) Exercise Pen Training

The exercise pen is a transition from kennel only training and will be helpful for those times when you may have to leave your puppy for more hours than they can reasonably be expected to hold it.

During those times when you must be away from the home for several hours, it's time to introduce your puppy to an exercise pen.

Exercise pens are usually constructed of wire sections that you can put together in whatever shape you desire, and the pen needs to be large enough to hold your puppy's kennel inside one half of the pen, while the other half will be lined with newspapers or pee pads.

Place your puppy's food and water dishes next to the kennel and leave the kennel door open, so they can wander in and out whenever they wish, to eat or drink or go to the papers or pads if they need to relieve themselves.

Your puppy will be contained in a small area of your home while you are away and because they are already used to sleeping inside their kennel, they will not want to relieve themselves inside the area where they sleep. Therefore, your puppy will naturally go to the other half of the pen to relieve themselves on the newspapers or pee pads.

This method will help train your puppy to be quickly "paper" trained when you must leave them alone for a few hours.

5) Puppy Apartment™ Training

A similar and more costly alternative, the *Puppy Apartment™* is a step up from the exercise pen training system that makes the process of crate or pen training even easier on both humans and puppies.

The Puppy Apartment™ works well in a variety of situations, whether you're at home and unable to pay close attention to your Kangal puppy's needs, whether you must be away from home for a few hours or during the evening when everyone is asleep and you don't particularly want to get up at 3:00 a.m. to take your puppy out to go pee.
The Puppy Apartment™ is an innovation that is convenient for both puppy and human alike.

What makes this system so effective is the patent pending dividing wall with a door leading to the other side, all inside the pen.

One side of the Puppy Apartment™ is where the puppy's bed is located and the other side (through the doorway) is the bathroom area that is lined with pee pads.

With the bathroom right next door, your puppy or dog can take a bathroom break whenever they wish, without the need to alert family members to let them out.

This one bedroom, one bathroom system, which is a combination of the kennel/training pen, is a great alternative for helping to eliminate the stress of worrying about always keeping a watchful eye on your puppy or getting up during the night to take them outside every few hours to help them avoid making mistakes.

According to Modern Puppies...

> *"The Puppy Apartment™ takes the MESSY out of paper training, the ODORS AND HASSLES out of artificial grass training, MISSING THE MARK out of potty pad training and HAVING TO HOLD IT out of crate training. House training a puppy has never been faster or easier!*
>
> *The Puppy Apartment™ has taken all the benefits of the most popular potty training methods and combined them into one magical device and potty training system. This device and system has revolutionized how modern puppies are potty trained!"*

Manufactured in the United States, this product ships directly from the California supplier (Modern Puppies).

Pricing of the Puppy Apartment™ begins at $138 / £80 and is only available online at Modern Puppies.

6) Free Training

If you would rather not confine your young puppy to one or two rooms in your home, and will be allowing them to freely range about your home anywhere they wish during the day, this is considered free training.

When free house training your puppy, you will need to closely watch your puppy's activities all day long so that you can be aware of the *"signs"* that will indicate when they need to go outside to relieve themselves.

For instance, circling and sniffing is a sure sign that they are looking for a place to do their business.

Never get upset or scold a puppy for having an accident inside the home, because this will result in teaching your puppy to be afraid of you and to only relieve themselves in secret places or when you're not watching.

If you catch your puppy making a mistake, all that is necessary is for you to calmly say *"No"*, and quickly scoop them up and take them outside or to their indoor bathroom area.

From your sensitive puppy's point of view, yelling or screaming when they make a potty mistake will be understood by your puppy or dog as unstable energy being displayed by the person who is supposed to be their leader. This type of unstable behaviour will only teach your puppy to fear and disrespect you.

When you are vigilant, the Kangal should not be a difficult puppy to housebreak and they will generally do very well when you start them off with *"puppy pee pads"* that you will move closer and closer to the same door that you always use when taking them outside. This way they will quickly learn to associate going to this door when they need to relieve themselves.

When you pay close attention to your puppy's sleeping, eating, drinking and playing habits, you will quickly learn their body language so that you are able to predict when they might need to relieve themselves.

Your puppy will always need to relieve themselves first thing in the morning, as soon as they wake up from a nap, approximately 20 minutes after they finish eating a meal, after they have finished a play session, and of course, before they go to bed at night.

It's important to have compassion during this house training time in your young Kangal's life so that their education will be as stress-free as possible.

It's also important to be vigilant because how well you pay attention will minimize the opportunities your puppy may have for making a bathroom mistake in the first place, and the fewer mistakes they make, the sooner your puppy will be house trained.

7) Mistakes Happen

Remember that a dog's sense of smell is at least 2,000 times more sensitive that our human sense of smell.

As a result of your puppy's superior sense of smell, it will be very important to effectively remove all odours from house training accidents, because otherwise, your puppy will be attracted by the smell to the place where they may have had a previous accident, and will want to do their business there again and again.

While there are many products that are supposed to remove odours and stains, many of these are not very effective. You want a professional grade cleaner that will not just mask one odour with another scent; you want a product that will completely neutralize odours.

TIP: go to RemoveUrineOdors.com and order yourself some *"SUN"* and/or *"Max Enzyme"* because these products contain professional-strength odour neutralizers and urine digesters that bind to and completely absorb odours on any type of surface.

8) Electronic Training Devices

Generally speaking, positive training methods are far more effective than using devices that involve negative stimulation.

Furthermore, unless you are training a Kangal to hunt badgers or rabbits, using electronic devices is usually an excuse for a lazy human who will not take the time to properly train their dog by teaching them rules and boundaries that lead to respect and an attentive follower.

When you do not provide your Kangal (or any dog) with a consistent leadership role that teaches your dog to trust, respect and listen to you in all circumstances, you will inevitably experience behavioural issues.

Electronic training devices such as e-collars, spray collars or electronic fencing all rely upon negative, painful or stressful reinforcement, which can easily cause your dog to become nervous or live a life of fear.

For instance, a dog simply cannot understand the principles of "invisible" boundaries, and therefore should never be subjected to the confusion of the punishment that occurs when walking across an invisible line within their own home territory.

Dogs naturally understand the positive training methods of receiving a reward, which is not only much more efficient and effective when teaching boundaries, rewards are far kinder, and create a much stronger bond with your dog.

a. The Truth About Shock Collars

First of all, it would have to be an extremely rare situation in which it would be necessary or recommended that you use a shock collar on a small Kangal as these devices are usually only employed in extreme situations, and generally for much larger breeds who could seriously harm someone.

The use of remote, electronic, shock or *"e-collars"* is at best a controversial subject that can quickly escalate into heated arguments.

In certain, rare circumstances, and when used correctly, the e-collar can be a helpful training tool that could actually save a dog's life if they are acting out in dangerous ways.

An e-collar would generally be utilized in a circumstance where a larger breed of dog has access to free range over a large property, resulting in difficulties getting their attention from a distance if they become distracted by other animals or smells.

Many dogs that have not been properly trained from a young age also learn that when they are off the leash and out of your immediate reach they can choose to ignore your commands, bark their heads off, terrorize the neighbours or chase wildlife.

All of these situations are generally not activities that a Kangal would have the slightest interest in because they love being at home with their humans.

Generally, e-collars can be effective training tools for working, herding, hunting or tracking dogs.

In these types of circumstances, a remote training collar can be an effective training device for reinforcing verbal commands from a great distance, such as "Come", "Sit" or "Stay".

Finally, electronic collars can be used as a last resort to help teach a dog not to engage in dangerous behaviour that could result in them being seriously harmed or even killed.

b. Electronic Fencing

Honestly, there are far more reasons NOT to install an electronic fence as a means of keeping your dog inside your yard, than there are good reasons for considering one.

For instance, a dog whose yard is surrounded by an electronic fence can quite easily develop fear, aggression, or both, directed towards what they may believe is the cause of the shock they are receiving.

As a result, installing an electronic fence may cause your dog to become aggressive toward cats, other dogs or other humans.

As well, a dog that receives a fright, or in excitement forgets about the shock they are going to receive, may run through an electronic fence and then be too frightened or stressed to come back home because it means that they must pass through the painful barrier again.

Another factor to keep in mind with respect to electronic fencing is that other dogs or teasing children can freely enter the yard and torment or attack your dog, and a thief bent on stealing your Kangal will be able to do so with ease.

The absolute best way to keep your dog safe in their own yard, while helping to establish your role as guardian and leader, is to be out there with them while they are on leash, and to only permit them freedom in your yard under your close supervision.

Chapter 6: Feeding

This is a daily chore. It is advised to feed Kangal dogs the best quality dog food available to you – branded dog foods are a plus.

Very important: ALWAYS make sure that your dog has access to clean water.

Human foods should be restricted to a bare minimum for your pets own good. Most dogs do not respond well to human food and may contract intestinal diseases. In worst-case scenarios, human foods can even cause poisoning in dogs!

Historically, Kangal dogs are known to have consumed barley meal, pita bread, and some fresh meat if available. They are believed to have hunted their food at times. This is the diet recognized by Kangal owners in their native city of Sivas, Turkey.

So, the more natural you try to keep its diet, the better it will be for your pet in the long run.

Foods like chocolate, tea, coffee, raisins, liquor, salty foods, unripe fruits and vegetables, tomato plant leaves, dough, onions, garlic and chives should *never* be given to a Kangal dog.

Most of these are known to have poisonous characteristics, which can seriously disrupt your Kangal dog's digestive system. In extreme cases, consuming these ingredients/foods can also cause lethal poisoning.

On the other hand, it ***may*** be given cottage cheese, certain fruits and vegetables, eggs and certain other foods but their quantities need to be regulated strictly. Too much human food can cause dental problems and a popular breath problem called halitosis.

Give your Kangal dog items that are especially made for it instead of treating them with bits of your own food.

The latter can lead to serious trouble and poisoning if you are unaware how Kangal dogs respond to different ingredients. It is better to be safe than sorry – feed it dog food and dog treats only.

As far as water is concerned, serve clean drinking water. Replace it often and clean the food and water bowls daily.

The health and well being of your puppy is in your hands, so don't let it slip.

On this note, also beware of protein-rich dog foods.

Use low protein dog foods for your Kangal dog to slow their growth slightly (although they will most probably grow up to the same size that is embedded in their genetic code).

Also try to look for organic dog foods instead of synthetic ones. The higher the quantity of chemicals, the more dangerous it will become for your pet.

This has been stressed multiple times already to emphasize the importance of choosing dog food smartly. It is the fundamental aspect of your Kangal dog's health. Being negligent about it can cost you severely in terms of your pet's health and well being.

Now, let's have a more detailed look in what and what not to feed your Kangal.

1) Feeding Puppies

For growing puppies, a general feeding rule of thumb is to feed 10% of the puppy's present body weight or between 2% and 3% of their projected adult weight each day.

Keep in mind that high energy puppies will require extra protein to help them grow and develop into healthy adult dogs, especially during their first two years of life. There are now many foods on the market that are formulated for all stages of a dog's life (including the puppy stage), so whether you choose one of these foods or a food specially formulated for puppies, they will need to be fed smaller meals more frequently throughout the day (3 or 4 times), until they are at least one year old.

NOTE: choose quality sources of meat protein for healthy puppies and dogs, including beef, buffalo, chicken, duck, fish, hare, lamb, ostrich, pork, rabbit, turkey, venison, or any other source of wild meaty protein.

2) Feeding Adults

An adult dog will generally need to be fed between 2% and 3% of their body weight each day. Read the labels and avoid foods that contain a high amount of grains and other fillers. Choose foods that list high quality meat protein as the main ingredient.

TIP: grated parmesan cheese sprinkled on a Kangal's dinner will help to stop picky eaters from ignoring their food. To get the cheese to stick to the kibble, first mix a small amount of olive oil into the kibble, and then sprinkle with finely grated Parmesan cheese.

3) Treats

Since the creation of the first dog treat over 150 years ago, the myriad of choices available on every pet store, feed store and grocery store shelf almost outnumbers those looking forward to eating them.

Today's treats are not just for making us guilty humans feel better because it makes us happy to give our furry friends something they really enjoy because today's treats are also designed to actually improve our dog's health.

Some of us humans treat our dogs just because, others use treats for training purposes, others for health, while others still treat for a combination of reasons.

For whatever reason you choose to give treats to your Kangal, keep in mind that if we treat our dogs too often throughout the day, we may create a picky eater who will no longer want to eat their regular meals. In addition, if the treats we are giving are high calorie, we may be putting our dog's health in jeopardy by allowing them to become overweight.

4) Treats to Avoid

a. Rawhide

Rawhide is soaked in an ash/lye solution to remove every particle of meat, fat and hair and then further soaked in bleach to remove remaining traces of the ash/lye solution. Now that the product is no longer food, it no longer has to comply with food regulations.

While the hide is still wet it is shaped into rawhide chews, and upon drying it shrinks to approximately 1/4 of its original size.

Furthermore, arsenic based products are often used as preservatives, and antibiotics and insecticides are added to kill bacteria that also fight against good bacteria in your dog's intestines.

The collagen fibres in the rawhide make it very tough and long lasting, which makes this chew a popular choice for humans to give to their dogs because it satisfies the dog's natural urge to chew while providing many hours of quiet entertainment. Sadly, when a dog chews a rawhide treat, they ingest many harsh chemicals and when your dog swallows a piece of rawhide, that piece can swell up to four times its size inside your dog's stomach, which can cause anything from mild to severe gastric blockages that could become life threatening and require surgery.

b. Pig's Ears

These treats are actually the ears of pigs, and while most dogs will eagerly devour them, they are extremely high in fat, which can cause stomach upsets, vomiting and diarrhoea for many dogs. Pig's ears are often processed and preserved with unhealthy chemicals that discerning dog guardians will not want to feed their dogs.

In addition, the ears are often quite thin and crispy and when the dog chews them pieces can break off, like chips, and can easily become stuck in a dog's throat.

While pig's ears are generally not considered to be a healthy treat choice for any dog, they should be especially avoided for any dog that may be at risk of being overweight.

c. Hoof Treats

Many humans give cow, horse and pig hooves to their dogs as treats because they consider them to be *"natural"*.

The truth is that after processing these *"treats"* they retain little, if any, of their *"natural"* qualities.

Hoof treats are processed with harsh preservatives, including insecticides, lead, bleach, arsenic based products, and antibiotics to kill bacteria, which can also harm the good bacteria in your dog's intestines, and if all bacteria is not killed in these meat based products before feeding them to your dog, they could also suffer from Salmonella poisoning.

Hooves can also cause chipping or breaking of your dog's teeth as well as perforation or blockages in your dog's intestines.

5) Healthy Treats

a. Hard Treats

There are so many choices of hard or crunchy treats available that come in many varieties of shapes, sizes and flavours, that you may have a difficult time choosing.

If your Kangal will eat them, hard treats will help to keep their teeth cleaner. Whatever you do choose, be certain to read the labels and make sure that the ingredients are high quality and appropriately sized for your Kangal friend.

b. Soft Treats

Soft, chewy treats are also available in a wide variety of flavours, shapes and sizes for all the different needs of our fur friends and are often used for training purposes as they have a stronger smell.

c. Dental Treats

Dental treats or chews are designed with the specific purpose of helping your Kangal to maintain healthy teeth and gums.

They usually require intensive chewing and are often shaped with high ridges and bumps to exercise the jaw and massage gums while removing plaque build-up near the gum line.

d. Freeze-Dried and Jerky Treats

Freeze-dried and jerky treats offer a tasty morsel most dogs find irresistible as they are usually made of simple, meaty ingredients, such as liver, poultry and seafood.

These treats are usually lightweight and easy to carry around, which means they can also be great as training treats.

e. Human Food Treats

You will want to be very careful when feeding human food to dogs as treats, because many of our foods contain additives and ingredients that could be toxic and harmful.

Be certain to choose simple, fresh foods with minimal or no processing, such as lean meat, poultry or seafood, and even if your Kangal will eat anything put in front of them, be aware that many common human foods, such as grapes, raisins, onions and chocolate are poisonous to dogs.

f. Training Treats

While any sort of treat can be used as an extra incentive during training sessions, soft treats are often used for training purposes because of their stronger smell and smaller sizes.

Yes, we humans love to treat our dogs, whether for helping to teach the new puppy to go pee outside, teaching the adolescent dog new commands, for trick training, for general good behaviour, or for no reason at all, other than that they just gave us the *"look"*.

Generally, the treats you feed your dog should not make up more than approximately 10% of their daily food intake, so make sure the treats you choose are high quality, so that you can help to keep your Kangal both happy and healthy.

6) Choosing the Right Food

In order to choose the right food for your Kangal, it's important to understand a little bit about canine physiology and what Mother Nature intended when she created our furry friends.

More than 230 years ago, in 1785, the English Sportman's dictionary described the best diet for a dog's health in an article entitled *"Dog"*.

This article indicated that the best food for a dog was something called *"Greaves"*, described as *"the sediment of melted tallow. It is made into cakes for dogs' food. In Scotland and parts of the US it is called cracklings."*

Out of the meagre beginning of the first commercially made dog food has sprung a massively lucrative and vastly confusing industry that has only recently begun to evolve beyond those early days of feeding our dogs the dregs of human leftovers because it was cheap and convenient for us humans.

Even today, the majority of dog food choices have far more to do with being convenient for humans to store and serve than it does with being a diet truly designed to be a nutritionally balanced, healthy food choice for a canine.
The dog food industry is big business and as such, because there are now almost limitless choices, there is much confusion and endless debate when it comes to answering the question, *"What is the best food for my dog?"*

Educating yourself by talking to experts and reading everything you can find on the subject, plus taking into consideration several relevant factors, will help to answer the dog food question for you and your dog.

For instance, where you live may dictate what sorts of foods you have access to. Other factors to consider will include the particular requirements of your dog, such as their age, energy and activity levels.

Next will be expense, time and quality. While we all want to give our dogs the best food possible, many humans lead very busy lives and cannot, for instance, prepare their own dog food, but still want to feed a high quality diet that fits within their budget. However, perhaps most important when choosing an appropriate diet for our dogs is learning to be more observant of Mother Nature's design and taking a closer look at our dog's teeth, jaws and digestive tract.

Our canine companions are carnivores, which means that they derive their energy and nutrient requirements from eating a diet consisting mainly or exclusively of the flesh of animal tissues (in other words, meat).

a. The Canine Teeth

The first part of your dog you will want to take a good look at when considering what to feed will be their teeth.

Unlike humans, who are equipped with wide, flat molars for grinding grains, vegetables and other plant-based materials, canine teeth are all pointed because they are designed to rip, shred and tear into animal meat and bone.

b. The Canine Jaw

Another obvious consideration when choosing an appropriate food source for our fur friends is the fact that every canine is born equipped with powerful jaws and neck muscles for the specific purpose of being able to pull down and tear apart their hunted prey.

The structure of the jaw of every canine is such that it opens widely to hold large pieces of meat and bone, while the actual mechanics of a dog's jaw permits only vertical (up and down) movement that is designed for crushing.

c. The Canine Digestive Tract

A dog's digestive tract is short and simple and designed to move their natural choice of food (hide, meat and bone) quickly through their systems.

Vegetables and plant matter require more time to break down in the gastrointestinal tract, which in turn requires a more complex digestive system than the canine body is equipped with.

The canine digestive system is simply unable to break down vegetable matter, which is why whole vegetables look pretty much the same going into your dog as they do coming out the other end.

Given the choice, most dogs would never choose to eat plants or vegetables and fruits over meat, however, we humans continue to feed them a kibble based diet that contains high amounts of vegetables, fruits and grains and low amounts of meat.

Plus, in order to get our dogs to eat fruits, vegetables and grains we usually have to flavour the food with meat or meat by-products.

How much healthier and long lived might our beloved fur friends be if, instead of largely ignoring nature's design for our canine companions, we chose to feed them whole, unprocessed, species-appropriate food?

With many hundreds of dog food brands to choose from, it's no wonder we humans are confused about what to feed our dogs to help them live long and healthy lives.

Below are some suggestions and questions that may help you choose a dog food company that you can feel comfortable with:

- How long have they have been in business?
- Is dog food their main industry?
- Are they dedicated to their brand?
- Are they easily accessible?
- Do they honestly answer your questions?
- Do they have a good Company Safety Standard?
- Do they set higher standards?
- Read the ingredients - where did they come from?
- Are the ingredients something you would eat?
- Are the ingredients farmed locally?
- Was it cooked using standards you would trust?
- Is the company certified under human food or organic guidelines?

Whatever you decide to feed your Kangal, keep in mind that, just as too much wheat, other grains and other fillers in our human diet is having detrimental effects on our human health, the same can be very true for our best fur friends.

Our dogs are also suffering from many of the same life threatening diseases that are rampant in our human society (heart disease, cancer) as a direct result of consuming a diet high in genetically altered, impure, processed and packaged foods.

7) The Raw Diet

While some of us believe we are killing ourselves as well as our dogs with processed foods, others believe that there are dangers in feeding raw food.

Those who are raw feeding advocates believe that the ideal diet for their dog is one which would be very similar to what a dog living in the wild would have access to hunting or foraging, and these canine guardians are often opposed to feeding their dog any sort of commercially manufactured pet foods, because they consider them to be poor substitutes.

On the other hand, those opposed to feeding their dogs a raw or biologically appropriate raw food diet believe that the risks associated with food-borne illnesses during the handling and feeding of raw meats outweigh the purported benefits.

Interestingly, even though the United States Food and Drug Administration (FDA) states that they do not advocate a raw diet for dogs, they do advise for those who wish to take this route, that following basic hygiene guidelines for handling raw meat can minimize any associated risks.

Furthermore, high pressure pasteurization (HPP), which is high pressure, water based technology for killing bacteria, is USDA-approved for use on organic and natural food products, and is being utilized by many commercial raw pet food manufacturers.

Interestingly, raw meats purchased at your local grocery store contain a much higher level of acceptable bacteria than raw food produced for dogs because the meat purchased for human consumption is supposed to be cooked, which will kill any bacteria that might be present.

This means that canine guardians feeding their dogs a raw food diet can be quite certain that commercially prepared raw foods sold in pet stores will be safer than raw meats purchased in grocery stores.

Many guardians of high energy, working breed dogs will agree that their dogs thrive on a raw or BARF (Biologically Appropriate Raw Food) diet and strongly believe that the potential benefits of feeding a raw dog food diet are many, including:

- Healthy, shiny coats
- Decreased shedding
- Fewer allergy problems
- Healthier skin
- Cleaner teeth
- Fresher breath
- Higher energy levels
- Improved digestion
- Smaller stools
- Strengthened immune system
- Increased mobility in arthritic pets
- Increase or improvement in overall health

All dogs, of every size, whether working breed or companion dogs are amazing athletes in their own right, therefore every dog deserves to be fed the best food available.

A raw diet is a direct evolution of what dogs ate before they became our domesticated pets and we turned toward commercially prepared, easy to serve dry dog food that required no special storage or preparation.

The BARF diet is all about feeding our dogs what they are designed to eat by returning them to their wild, evolutionary diet.

8) The Dehydrated Diet

Dehydrated dog food comes in both raw meat and cooked meat forms and these foods are usually air dried to reduce moisture to the level where bacterial growth is inhibited.

The appearance of de-hydrated dog food is very similar to dry kibble and the typical feeding methods include adding warm water before serving, which makes this type of diet both healthy for our dogs and convenient for us to serve.

Dehydrated recipes are made from minimally processed fresh whole foods to create a healthy and nutritionally balanced meal that will meet or exceed the dietary requirements of a healthy canine.

Dehydrating removes only the moisture from the fresh ingredients, which usually means that because the food has not already been cooked at a high temperature, more of the overall nutrition is retained.

A de-hydrated diet is a convenient way to feed your dog a nutritious diet because all you have to do is add warm water, and wait five minutes while the food re-hydrates so your Kangal can enjoy a warm meal.

9) The Kibble Diet

While many canine guardians are starting to take a closer look at the food choices they are making for their furry companions, there is no mistaking that the convenience and relative economy of dry dog food kibble, that had its beginnings in the 1940's, continues to be the most popular pet food choice for most dog friendly humans.

Some 75 years later, the massive pet food industry offers up a confusingly large number of choices with hundreds of different manufacturers and brand names lining the shelves of veterinarian offices, grocery stores and pet food aisles.

While feeding a high quality bagged kibble diet that has been flavoured to appeal to dogs and supplemented with vegetables and fruits to appeal to humans may keep almost every Kangal companion happy and relatively healthy, you will ultimately need to decide whether this is the best diet for them.

10) Frequency of Feeding

In case you have brought home a puppy, keep in mind that the frequency of their meals will be higher – up to four times per day.

During their second quarter, you can reduce this frequency to three times per day.

You can further reduce it to two meals in a day during the third and fourth quarter of its first year.

Once it has hit the one-year benchmark, it is likely to shift over to one substantial meal in a day.

Some Kangal dogs prefer consuming two smaller meals instead of one large one. You will need to see through your pet's preferences and serve it accordingly for best growth.

11) The Right Bowl

Below is a brief description of the different categories and types of dog bowls that would be appropriate choices for your Kangal's particular needs:

Automatic Watering Bowls: are standard dog bowls (often made out of plastic) that are attached to a reservoir container, which is designed to keep water constantly available to your dog as long as there is water remaining in the storage compartment.

Ceramic/Stoneware Bowls: an excellent choice for those who like options in personality, colour and shape.

Elevated Bowls: raised dining table dog bowls are a tidy and classy choice that will make your dog's dinner time a more comfortable experience while getting the bowls off the floor.

No Skid Bowls: are for dogs that push their bowls across the floor when eating. A non-skid dog bowl will help keep the feed bowl where you put it.

No Tip Bowls: are designed to prevent the messy type of doggy eater from flipping over their dinner or water bowls.

Stainless Steel Bowls: are as close to indestructible as a bowl can be, plus they are sanitary, easy to clean and water stays cooler for a longer period of time in a stainless bowl.

Wooden Bowls: for those humans concerned about stylish home decor, wooden dog bowl dining stations are beautiful pieces of furniture unto themselves that can enhance your home decor.

Travel Bowls: are convenient, practical and handy additions for every canine travel kit.

Consider a space saving, collapsible dog bowl, made out of hygienic, renewable bamboo that comes in fun colours and different sizes, making it perfect for every travel bowl needs.

If you would like to learn more about all the many dog bowl choices available, visit DogBowlForYourDog.com, which is a comprehensive, one-stop website dedicated to explaining the ins and outs of every food bowl imaginable and helping you find the perfect bowl for all your Kangal's needs.

Chapter 7: Caring for Your Kangal Dog

If it looks promising to you at this point, the rest will not be much of a problem.

Every dog has its own set of pampering needs and the same is the case with the Kangal dog. If you have the power to live with the aforementioned characteristics of the Kangal breed, the rest will automatically follow.

Here are a few pointers about how you can take care of your Kangal dog and promote this association for greater gains.

It is important to keep in mind that whatever you do for your pet and how well you care for it will not only reflect on your pet's physical grooming and well-being but also on its personality development. So make the best choices for a Kangal dog that makes you proud.

1) Grooming

Everyone likes to see a dog that is well kept. The Kangal breed is no exception to this. Here are a few grooming essentials particular to the Kangal breed, which will help you make your Kangal dog look its best at all times. It just needs a little bit of effort and dedication from your end.

a. The Coat

The Kangal breed possesses double coats – the undercoat is short and dense while the overcoat has long, coarser hairs. This does not only help in keeping the canine warm during winters but also helps in protecting the body against bites from stray animals.

Generally, you will need to brush your Kangal dog's coat twice a week to keep it free from tangles. However, the Kangal breed is known to shed their coat heavily twice a year – most heavily during the summer months. This is absolutely normal and helps thicker hair to grow later on during the winter season.

Brushing the coat stimulates the nerves and blood vessels present underneath the skin. This automatically helps in improving the quality of hair that grows later on. Therefore, remember to brush your pet's hair every now and then – even if it apparently seems to be going bald.

Witnessing Kangal dog's hair fall year round is not exactly uncommon. So you need not get worried about it if your Kangal does that. In fact, bald patches on its coat are also considered normal. Over time, these bald patches will be covered with hair as the winter season approaches.

Make sure you use reliable products for grooming and brush its hair regularly to keep the mess to a minimum. The quality of grooming essentials is also an important factor in determining the health of the Kangal dog's coat. Look around for high quality and reliable products. Seek advice from the veterinary doctor if required. Don't forget to use a flea brush on your pet every once in a while to free it from these notorious pests. Your Kangal dog's playful "outdoor" nature is likely to get it into a lot of medical issues. Keep a close check on these and have regular consultations with a vet.

Keep in mind that brushing its coat does not only help in improving the quality of its hair but also helps in bonding. So take your time to pamper your newfound friend – it loves your attention.

b. The Nails

If left to pursue its natural course of life, you will not need to trim the nails of a Kangal dog. Its vigorous hunting lifestyle causes adequate wearing of the nails continuously and naturally. However, in home life, you will need to do it at least once a month depending on its growth rate.

Use trimmers instead of clippers to avoid hurting your dog. Leave ample distance between the pink area of its paw and the final length of its nails. Once hurt, it will not be very enthusiastic about the clipping process, so be careful. It is best to have a companion by your side to control the dog's movements.

You can use nail clippers as well provided you know how to use these and not hurt your pet. If unsure, cut the nail in small pieces and look underneath to see where the flesh begins. Don't be in a hurry – you might end up doing it wrong.

On the same note, don't wait too long to clip your Kangal dog's nails. This is one part of the body that grows rapidly. Unless you have a contingency plan to control the degree of scratches and injuries it is likely to inflict on you and others while exhibiting its love, remember to clip its nails at least once in a month.

c. Dental Hygiene

Yes, your dog needs regular brushing as well. Bad breath and inadequate dental hygiene can eventually lead to bigger problems – including upset stomach and halitosis. Make sure you brush your pet's teeth every day (or every few days).

You can use commercially produced products or use homemade ones by combining baking soda with water. Use soft nylon cloth or commercial toothbrushes to clean its teeth. Don't agitate your pet, as its teeth are the last place you want to be near to while it is angry.

Inability to do so can lead your Kangal dog towards gum diseases that can aggravate into teeth-loss. Keep your dog's smile healthy – brush its teeth and gums regularly.

Have its teeth and gums regularly inspected by the veterinary doctor. This will help in diagnosing a problem at the earliest. Consequently, it will be easier to devise a plan of action to overcome this problem in a timely manner.

d. The Ears

Have your Kangal checked regularly for ear infections. Ear cropping (covered under a subsequent heading) does not prevent ear infections. This becomes more important once your Kangal has had its periodic bath.

You can find a number of chemical solutions on the market to clean your pet's ears. Make sure you've consulted the veterinarian before using any.

Also seek advice from your veterinary doctor to find out how best to clean your canine's ears. Too much debris can build up into a major health problem. Most evidently though, too much debris can lead to loss of hearing, which might be misinterpreted as lack of obedience.

Do yourself and your Kangal dog a favour; clean its ears regularly, so you can nurture a well-rounded relationship with your pet.

e. The Bath

Kangal dogs do not need frequent bathing. So doing it once every month is sufficient.

You can bathe it more often if your Kangal has a knack of getting into places that are not meant for it. Use good quality dog shampoos and conditioners to bathe it.

Do ask your veterinarian for advice. Some shampoos work best on hair fall and coat shine. Follow the expert's advice instead of commercials and advertisements for best results.

Keep in mind that a shiny, healthy coat is not only associated with the use of good products but also with its diet. So if the medicated (or non-medicated) shampoos do not seem to work, it is most probably because the problem lies elsewhere.

Its eyes, genitals and facial area are sensitive. Do not apply any chemicals on these parts. Use water to wash these.

Once bathed – it will take about half an hour to damp, rub, scrub and wash its coat – let it shake off excess water naturally. Make sure its coat is dry to avoid picking up dirt and dust and to prevent infestations such as fleas.

If it is the shedding season, be prepared to collect the hairs in the bath, on the bath towel and other accessories. They have the tendency to become a nuisance around the house.

The general rule of thumb says having a pet automatically mandates a certain degree of disorder. Expect to see dog hair in uncanny places. There may be a few spots and stains involved as well. As a dog enthusiast, such observations should become a norm for you.

If you are too uptight about cleanliness, then probably getting a pet dog is not a very good idea after all!

2) Tail Docking/Ear Cropping

The Kangal dog usually has a long, curled up tail and drooping ears over its wide head. This is how it is born and it naturally exists.

Most Kangal enthusiasts believe that tail docking or ear clipping is not necessary. It distorts the natural image of the breed and is not known to yield any positive results as such. In fact, initiatives around the country are being promoted to discourage these activities as they are purely done for cosmetic reasons.

a. Why Not?

Some believe tail docking (removal of the dog's tail) and ear cropping (removal of the dog's ears – in part or in full) is done to improve the Kangal dog's responses.

Tail docking puts it at an advantage against the enemy, as the Kangal does not have this imminent weakness. Ear cropping is believed to help Kangal dogs hear better and avoid ear infections.

To date, there is no evidence to support these convictions and hence it does not justify putting your beloved pet through all the pain and trouble to modify its appearance.

On top of this, having the tail docked in full consciousness (since the puppies are not given anaesthesia for this purpose) and the ears cropped (under aesthetic influence) is a substantial threat to the canine's well being.

The risk of permanent sedation, infection, improper healing, and excessive blood loss is present. So it is recommended not to go for these practices that put your pet in unnecessary pain.

b. The Modern Point of View

Nowadays, tail docking and ear cropping is frowned upon and may even cause you to lose your pedigree registration on the basis of disqualification. Experts have come to the conclusion that either of these activities have no medicinal benefits and are done for cosmetic reasons only. Consequently, the validity of most claims has been officially lost.

Weigh all odds properly before pursuing this course of action – there are no benefits to it but a lot that can be lost. Keep in mind that your Kangal dog has nothing to gain by going through these gruesome procedures. So why put it through it when there is nothing to be won?

The idea behind adopting a Kangal dog is to offer it a home worth living in. In exchange, you get the companionship of a truly loyal canine friend.

Stick to the purpose and you would not need to get into such surgical procedures.

3) Worming

The Kangal dog can fall prey to numerous worm infestations like hookworms, roundworms, heartworms and several others. This is attributable to its rural lifestyle. It is recommended that you should get your Kangal dog scrutinized for worms once every year.

If your pet has fallen ill and shows some signs of trouble, do not hesitate to visit a veterinarian. Whenever identified, you will need to administer certain specific medications to your Kangal so that the worms can be eliminated.

Keep in mind that all worms do not respond the same way to medications. You will need to make sure you are using the right medicine for the right kind of infestation in order to eliminate the problem entirely.

Keep the contact number of a professional veterinary doctor handy. Also draft up a schedule for regular check-ups and stick to it.

Apart from worms, your Kangal dog is prone to a number of other complications – DHLPP for instance. Have your pet regularly screened for signs of medical complications in order to resolve them in a timely manner.

If left unattended for long, they may become lethal for your companion. Be proactive about its needs and offer timely medical assistance. It will help prolong the life of your canine friend for a truly fulfilling journey ahead.

4) Accommodation

Kangal dogs are huge, so naturally they need a lot of space. However, in more specific terms, this section can be sorted out into the following three sections:

a. The Sleep Zone

The Kangal dog likes it quiet and peaceful during the night. So keeping its bed in the living room is probably not a very good idea. Designate a separate, secluded space for the Kangal to enjoy its sleep.

On this note, it is worth mentioning that the Kangal breed is nocturnal by nature, that is, they are active and awake through the night.

So if you are trying to put it to sleep at night time, it will take some training to achieve.

The slightest hint of some noise can alert the Kangal dog – an act that is most likely to be followed by incessant barking.

This adequately summarizes the importance of silence in their sleep area.

b. The Activity Zone

The Kangal dog loves large open spaces. Keeping it locked up in small places (like an apartment) is likely to be accompanied with obnoxious behaviour on behalf of the dog – like torn sofas, chewed up cushions, broken furniture and others.

Make sure you give it the liberty of open space for at least a portion of the day.

If you have a backyard, let it explore this area but do remember to cordon off your flowerbeds. Take it out for a walk multiple times during the day so it does not feel cramped.

c. The Social Space

The Kangal dog needs to be socialized in order to make it friendlier towards strangers.

Make sure you never leave it off the leash during these sessions. Skirmishes can attract their attention and may lead to aggravated assaults if the Kangal is let off the collar.

Let it around different people and other animals but make sure to keep a close eye on its progress.

It is extremely protective of its lot by nature. So if you (or someone from your home) get into a tug-of-war (even for fun) your Kangal dog will recognize it as threat and attack your opponent. Be careful around your pet – especially if it is in the initial phases of training.

Training clubs and socialization centres are a good place to begin. Make sure you do not push your Kangal dog too hard to become social. Let it adjust and adapt one step at a time.

d. The Guardian's Lifestyle

The aforementioned arrangements will work if you are trying to help the Kangal dog become your companion. However, the real lifestyle of this guardian dog is in the wild.

It lives and sleeps outdoors. It is usually more vigilant and active during the night and a little subdued during the morning hours.

It likes being given responsibility instead of being entertained with recreational activities. You can even consider it to be a workaholic.

Regardless of whether you build a dog shed for it or not, it is likely to stay near its "flock" at all times.

It doesn't need a lot of luxury or comfort; rather, it is built for the rural life. If you can offer your pet with such a lifestyle, you will not be disappointed with its performance.

5) Playtime

Every dog needs some regular playtime each day, and this is even more important with an active breed, such as the Kangal, who will be your loving, energetic companion.

While every Kangal will be different with respect to what types of games they may enjoy, most Kangal's will enjoy a game of fetch with a ball or chasing a Frisbee, and some may even enjoy swimming to retrieve a stick.

A fun game of *"Search"*, where you ask your Kangal to "Sit/Stay" while you hide a favourite treat that they then have to find, will appeal to the Kangal's ancient hunting instincts.

After a disciplined walk with your Kangal, they will also enjoy being given the opportunity for some off leash freedom to run. Play and socialize with other similar sized dogs.

6) Setting the Rules

The Kangal breed (and all other dog breeds for that matter) has a built-in tendency to believe they are the leaders. It comes as their natural instinct. You therefore need to establish your supremacy over your pet from day one to make it subservient to you.

Never let the Kangal dog lead. Always enter your home before the dog.

In fact, all family members should enter the house before the Kangal to set its place. While leaving the house or entering it, humans should be the ones leading instead of the canines.

Secondly, feed yourself before feeding your pet. This simple act will also help in defining its place in the hierarchy. If you serve it its food before eating yourself, it will wrongly lead it to believe it has ruled.

Moreover, if you find the Kangal dog blocking your way at some time, make sure you instruct it to move instead of going around this hurdle.

The king does not change places – so if you do the latter, you are reinforcing its instincts. Motion the Kangal dog to move and use disciplinary actions if required. Every small act on your behalf is building an image in your pet's mind.

Last but not least, never let the Kangal dog sleep in your bed with you. It may look brutal or rude or against the laws of love, but rest assured this isn't the case.

By giving your dog a special designated space and making sure it sleeps nowhere but there, you are in fact controlling its behaviour. In the long run, these actions will help in building a mutually beneficial companionship.

On this note, keep in mind that the Kangal breed is exceptionally stubborn. It will not adjust easily with your dominating nature. There may be a few problems here and there. But if you let the Kangal dog be, as it wants to be, rest assured it is a sure recipe for disaster.

Do yourself and your pet a favour – set the rules and make sure your Kangal follows them. It will eventually help in training your pet at a later stage.

7) Transporting

Travel crates are easily the best option available to transport your pet. Make sure it has ample space inside to move a little. Kangal dogs, seeing their size, will readily grow too big for travel crates. In this case, the next best option for you is to employ your personal car.

Public transport, though not really prohibited, will not be a very good idea considering its protective nature. If the place is not too far away, walk your canine companion to its destination. If this isn't possible, avoid putting other people's lives in danger and use your car instead.

Your car might need a few adjustments to accommodate your pet. Nevertheless, it is an investment worth making – especially if you are a frequent traveller.

Remember to add in identification documents to your dog's collar before leaving home and put it on a leash wherever possible. Keep the windows rolled up so your Kangal does not feel the impulse to escape.

Also try to keep it on the back seat to prevent it from interfering with your driving. The ideal scenario is to have someone holding the dog and keeping it distracted.

Movement excites Kangal dogs. So naturally having blinds or some toys to keep its eyes away from the windows will be a good idea.

Know how your pet signals the call of nature. You definitely do not want reminders of the trip in your car.

Take frequent breaks and walk the Kangal dog to exhaust its energy reserves. A tired Kangal is easier to control compared to one that is full of energy. Improvise along the way as and when required.

There are no hard and fast principles – go with your gut instincts and you should be fine.

After the first few visits, you will automatically find out what more needs to be done to facilitate travels. It isn't a one-time affair. So we suggest you adapt to the rising needs with time.

8) Possible Illnesses and Plan of Action

The Kangal breed is comparatively "free" from health problems. There are no particular genetic problems associated with this breed.

There have been cases where incidence of hip dysplasia, dermatologic musculoskeletal lipomas and other similar "dog" problems were observed but these are extremely rare.

On the other hand, halitosis is quite rampant among this breed.

Bad breath can prove to be quite challenging to tackle, especially if your pet loves to lick you. The most appropriate plan of action for this issue is to take your dog in for a dental check-up.

Frequent teeth brushing and use of medicated toothpastes can usually solve this problem within a month. Ask for expert advice on this issue to make sure there are no other problems attached to it.

If your pet shows signs of trouble while walking or digesting food, take it to a veterinary doctor at the earliest.

Do not allow it to run on slippery surfaces as it can damage the cartilage in its paws and knees.

Stick to its periodic check-up schedule to identify problems right when they begin to emerge. It is the only plan of action that can keep your Kangal dog safe from medical problems.

9) Vaccinations

This has been covered in ample detail previously. So here is a little recap.

Your Kangal dog needs to be protected against quite a few diseases right from puppyhood. It is the same way humans protect their children against imminent medical problems.

For Kangal puppies, the inoculations include prevention against Canine Distemper, Parainfluenza, Parovirus, Leptospirosis, Hepatitis, Rabies, Corona and Bordatella. The first five of these are commonly injected as a combination vaccine by the name of DHLPP.

The inoculations are administered in the second, third and fourth month of the puppy's life. From then on, the frequency is reduced to once a year.

If you have a Kangal dog older than four months' old that has not been vaccinated yet, it would be given two shots back-to-back with a difference of three weeks at max. Then, the frequency of vaccinations will be tuned down to once a year. At your first visit to the vet, you will be handed a chart/schedule for your companion's periodic vaccinations. Make sure you put reminders so that you do not miss out on these important dates.

Protect your canine companion – get it vaccinated regularly!

10) Safety Measures

There are two extremely important things you need to do – preferably before bringing your pet home. It is for the sake of your Kangal dog's own safety, so try not to leave it off for a later date. For all you know, disaster may already have struck by then.

Here is what you need to do:

a. Fencing

Make sure they are tall, sturdy and properly fixed.

You'll need them to be higher than six feet as a full grown Kangal dog can easily jump up to this height (most not-so-fully-grown will be able to achieve this benchmark just as well).

The smallest of sounds can tick off a Kangal dog and put it in pursuit of the source. So imagine what a stray dog could do.

Put fences in place to contain the Kangal dog within the premises.

Most people in your neighbourhood will not be very cool about a large dog on the loose. If you can afford it and you have a large space in your house, try to keep your Kangal dog indoors.

If not then the least you can do is install good quality fences.

Keep an eye on any suspicious craters underneath the fence. They are intelligent beings and know how to get around rules. You will need to be smarter to keep it safe.

b. Non-Slip Surfaces

As puppies, the Kangal dog is as playful as a toddler. It loves to run around your house and explore things that are deliberately kept away from plain view.

While it sprints, it can easily slip on polished floors and tiles that do not offer adequate grip for its soft paws.

It may apparently look endearing to see a small puppy slipping across the floor. But the fact is that this action is detrimental for its paws and knees.

The cartilage gets damaged, which may pave the way for arthritis and other problems later on in its life. Save it from avoidable miseries and install a non-slip carpet in your house – especially in those areas that the Kangal dog is allowed to explore.

Keep those little paws safe so your guardian dog can serve its purpose.

c. Dog-Proofing

It has already been covered in adequate detail previously. Sift through the previous pages of this book to find out all about dog-proofing your house.

12) Breeding

Would you like to breed Kangal dogs and raise your own family of companion guardian dogs?

Make sure you check in with the local law to see if there are legalities you need to fulfil before indulging in your passion. Once the legalities have been taken care of, the next most important thing is deciding how to go about this phase.

Generally, when you approach breeders to purchase a Kangal dog for a companion, they will include a clause in the contract, which obliges you to get your mate spayed or neutered once it has matured – usually within one to four years.

This is done to protect the sanctity of the Kangal breed and to prevent crossbreeding or breeding using unhealthy or unfit animals.

There are a lot of intricacies involved in this process. If you don't have a clear idea about what needs to be done and how, it is best left up to the experts.

All over the world, the importance of finding the right mates for breeding has been recognized and appreciated. The genuine breeder will be able to provide you with documents that say the parents are healthy and fit for breeding.

Any specimen that does not meet the given guidelines is disqualified from the pedigree champion line (and hence considered unfit for breeding purposes).

Wisely chosen partners automatically translate into better-behaved litters. Selecting partners at random or inbreeding can cause severe disturbances in the personalities of the litters.

The Kangal breed is capable of producing five to ten puppies at a time.

Historically, due to the geographical seclusion from other breeds, the Kangal dogs have preserved a fine, distinctive gene pool.

The Turkish authorities and dog clubs all around the world are working vigorously to protect the sanctity of different dog breeds and to achieve their champion lineage. The Kangal dog is no exception and hence it is recommended not to breach this trust by attempting to breed your pet at home.

However, if you have two certified purebred Kangal dogs of opposite genders available to you and there are no legal implications you will need to face, you can go for breeding them.

Make sure to get the litter registered as well. It will not only add value to the litter but also develop your credibility in the local community.

Search for viable homes to get the offspring adopted if you do not plan to keep them on site for long.

Keep in mind that breeding the Kangal dog every time it gets in heat will not only impact its health but also that of its litter. Make sure there is ample duration between the litters to ensure quality.

In fact, most clubs will deny registrations if the dam has already given birth to four litters.

While breeding, take exceptionally good care of the parents (especially the mother) to ensure healthy and happy puppies.

13) Walking

Kangal dogs need more than two hours' exercise daily to stay fit and healthy. Puppies will need shorter durations according to their stamina and age. Remember never to push your pet too hard to meet goals. You might end up damaging its mental and physical health.

Walking your Kangal dog should be a mix of slow walk, brisk walk, jog, and run – to stimulate its bones, ligaments and muscles in a 360° fashion.

At all times, never let the Kangal lead your way. You should be the one in the lead to establish your leadership over the canine. Have it bow on your heels if you are planning to halt for a few minutes to catch your breath.

Never use any machines to stimulate its walk. Let it run naturally on the ground as this will help develop its natural instincts. Artificial floors can cause slipping and other injuries.

Preferably, walk your Kangal dog in gardens and other green areas. Let it socialize with other people and animals but don't let it get too close.

Keep in mind that the Kangal dog is a large sized breed and hence might prove to be intimidating to others. If you want to promote its friendly side, keep its ferocious getup at home.

A single, long walk is appreciated, though you can settle for two short ones too. Make sure you exhaust its energy reserves adequately to keep your property safe from its wrath.

Only when your pet proves to be extremely well behaved and disciplined should you think about letting it off its leash. Don't be in any hurry to do so. You never know when your Kangal dog starts thinking otherwise!

14) Spaying and Neutering

If you do not intend to breed your Kangal dogs then spaying the female ones and neutering the male dogs is recommended. It is a big favour to the species as it then rids them from their periodic heat cycles.

Spaying and neutering are the terms used to describe the act of removing an animal's genitals.

The Kangal dog will no longer able to play its role in furthering the breed. This also effectively puts an end to their reproductive cycles – a blessing considering the mess and agitation they tend to be in during this time period.

It is a surgical process that is usually performed under the influence of general anaesthesia.

For the males, the testicles are removed which efficiently solves their problem.

For the females, an incision is made to remove the ovaries and uterus.

The risks pertaining to surgical procedures exist like the risk of contracting infections, not recovering from anaesthetic influence or excessive blood loss. It therefore needs extensive evaluation to ensure the procedure is carried out as safely as possible.

Spaying and neutering pets (any type of pet for that matter) is a debatable question that has ruled the discussion forums for quite some time now. It's a controversial topic but those in favour of spaying and neutering believe it is important to control their behaviour and also to practice pure breeding. In either case, here is what you need to know about spaying and neutering Kangal dogs.

For the male Kangal dogs, it is advised to wait for up to one year. The sexual hormones in Kangal dogs are not only responsible for reproduction but for their physical maturation as well.

If you neuter the male before it hits maturity, you might end up with a dog that does not meet the typical "guardian" standards of a Kangal dog.

By the end of its first year, most of its physical features resemble those of a fully-grown and hence this is the ideal time to get it neutered.

For the female Kangal dogs, however, it tends to be slightly more complicated. The female ones are likely to hit their first cycle when they are between the age of 9 months and 14 months. It can become really a handful to control these creatures during this time period.

You will need to keep it locked down and away from sight in a place from where it cannot get out and other dogs cannot get in.

On top of this, they are likely to discharge sickly liquids from their privates owing to their aroused situation. Coupled with their agitation, this translates into a whole lot of mess – even in places you would prefer to keep clean.

The bloody discharges are typical of their maturation (or coming in heat) and hence not something to worry about. However, they do signal the time when your pet needs to be kept secluded to avoid contact with other dogs.

Some dogs bleed profusely while some exhibit stains. Using clothing of some kind or dog pads will help you keep your furniture clean.

For this reason most people prefer to get female Kangal dogs spayed before they hit puberty or reach the age of 9 months.

However, some believe it is preferable to let them go through their first cycle before getting them spayed. In the end, the decision is yours – as long as the veterinary doctor says your pet will be fine in either case.

Some breeders will have the puppies spayed and neutered well before delivering them to their owners. This is done to discourage unprofessional breeding.

If this is not the case, the contract you sign before gaining the official ownership of your dog may contain a clause that compels you to get the animal spayed or neutered when it comes to a certain age. Breeders may do so to quench competition as well.

Make sure you read the fine print well before entering into the deal to prevent future heartbreaks. Also evaluate your decision to breed or not to breed carefully – once spayed or neutered, the dog will become infertile for life.

It is a shame to put an end to champion lineage. Discuss these matters closely with your breeder as well as the veterinary doctor to get matters cleared beforehand.

Ethically and humanely, it is a wrong deed to bring a generation to a standstill for your personal convenience. At the same time, it is a necessity to control your pet's agitated behaviours and restlessness.

Your pet is likely to go through the cycle time and time again throughout its decade long life. Apparent brutality might seem justified in the face of the pain your pet goes through each time.

Even so, take time to evaluate the odds. Improvise and develop solutions to your problems. If you have a viable solution – like a settlement with your breeder for instance – play your role in preserving the Kangal pedigree.

a. Benefits of Spaying and Neutering

Spaying and neutering have their own set of benefits and potential disadvantages. Here is what you need to know to make a well-informed decision in this regard:

1. It ends their periodic pains.
Yes, it is painful for your pet when it comes to heat but is kept away from mating for whatever reason. You may do so to prevent cross breeding or for some other reasons of your own. Nevertheless, spaying and neutering relieves your pet from these frequent pains for a better and peaceful life.

2. It makes them calmer and more loving.
It has been observed that pets that have been spayed or neutered tend to be more compassionate with their owners compared to those who are left to their natural selves and then restrained from mating.
It is related to their pain and the apparent loss of control whenever the Kangal dog becomes aroused.

3. It keeps them healthier.
A dog that has not been spayed or neutered is prone to a wide array of health problems like sexual diseases, infections, cancers and others.
Once sterilized, your pet is likely to lead a fuller, healthier and better life. In fact, dogs that are sterilized before hitting puberty are likely to combat these problems in a better way.
It is therefore advised to have your pet spayed or neutered while it is in its puppyhood.

4. No risk of unintentional breeding.
It is relatively easier and affordable to maintain a single pet. But when it comes to maintaining their family, it can greatly aggravate the situation.
Most people do not have the resources to house an entire family

of dogs.
Contrary to popular belief, finding new homes for the puppies is not as easy as it seems. Not everyone is on the lookout for puppies and hence having seven to eight littermates adopted within the first year is a long shot.
Moreover, the initial costs of upkeep are also likely to be quite high as for the first 8 weeks puppies need to remain near their biological mothers.
If the Kangal dog develops complications while giving birth, it will open a whole new chapter of problems and worries that can be associated with unintentional breeding.

If at this point you are convinced about the potential benefits of spaying and neutering, read through the next section to understand the dangers you put your pet through when you decide to have it spayed or neutered.

b. Disadvantages of Spaying and Neutering

Here is the other side of the picture that you need to see before making a decision. It is not a small verdict to make – your pet's life depends on it.

It is therefore in your best interests to evaluate the pros and cons properly before proceeding with your choice.

1. Surgical risks are involved.
Your pet will be under the influence of general anaesthesia so that it does not feel the pain of being sterilized.
Consequently, there are chances your pet might not be able to recover from the effects of anaesthesia or that some other complication may arise.
This is one of the biggest reasons why spaying and neutering has not been legally enforced. You might end up accidently euthanizing your pet against your will as you try to resolve its reproductive issues.

2. Breeding cannot occur.
If at a future point in time you decide you have the resources and the ability to house your pet's family, this will not be possible. Spaying and neutering sterilizes your pet, makes it infertile and hence unable to parent a generation. So if there is even the slightest chance you might want to see its offspring, you should not get it sterilized.
Spaying and neutering is done to prevent overpopulation of pets – a phenomenon that recently came into light with the rising numbers of euthanized animals.
In a way, if you are against cross breeding and euthanasia, having your pet spayed or neutered is better. You are able to play your part in preserving the pedigree lineage for your pet and also in controlling unwanted pet population.

3. It alters the appearance.
The reproductive hormones in Kangal dogs are not only responsible for their primary function. Instead, reproductive hormones also play a role in the dog's physical maturation.
So when they are sterilized, their appearance may change accordingly.
Both male and female dogs are likely to gain some weight after being spayed or neutered. This is most probably linked with the way their body apportions its energy reserves to maintain the proper functioning of its systems.
On the other hand, the absence of testicles for the male Kangal can be an issue. As your pet lacks the obvious signs of masculinity, it may become a source of ridicule and pun in your social circles.
Make sure you consult your veterinary doctor on the topic of cosmetic implants to retain your Kangal dog's manhood.

Once you have read through the benefits and disadvantages stated in here, you will know that it is a tricky decision. It is not inclined to any one dimension; rather, you need to evaluate and weigh up the options carefully to decide what is best for you and for your pet.

Regardless of what you decide, rest assured your pet will love you just the same. There are a lot of aspects in action when it comes to spaying or neutering.

If you are caring for your pet in the right way, there is no reason why this would become a source of contempt in your relationship with your Kangal dog.

Take your time to make a decision and make sure it is not influenced by temporary circumstances. When you have decided, just go for it.

Chapter 8: Socializing

Most Kangals are naturally friendly and social dogs, however, they will still need to be exposed to different people, places and unusual sights and sounds when they are puppies.

Any dog that is not regularly socialized may become shy or suspicious of unfamiliar or unusual people or circumstances, which could lead to nervous or fearful behaviour.

1) With Other Dogs and Pets

Generally speaking, the majority of an adult dog's habits and behavioural traits will be formed between the ages of birth and one year old.

This is why it will be very important to introduce your Kangal puppy to a wide variety of locations, sights, sounds, smells and situations during this formative period in their young life.

Your Kangal puppy will learn how to behave, in all these various circumstances, by following your lead, feeling your energy and watching how you react in every situation.

For instance, never accidentally reward your Kangal puppy or dog for displaying nervousness, fear or growling at another dog or person by picking them up.

Picking up a Kangal puppy or dog at this time, when they are displaying unbalanced energy, actually turns out to be a reward for them, and you will be teaching them to continue with this type of behaviour.

In addition, picking up a puppy literally places them in a top dog position, where they have the higher ground and literally become more dominant than the person or dog they may have just growled at.

The correct action to take in such a situation is to gently correct your Kangal puppy, with a firm, yet calm energy by distracting them with a "no", or a quick sideways snap of the leash to get their attention back on you, so that they learn to let you deal with the situation on their behalf.

If you allow a fearful, nervous or shy puppy deal with situations that unnerve them without your direction, they may learn to react with fear or aggression to unfamiliar circumstances and you will have created a problem that could escalate into something quite serious as they grow older.

The same is true of situations where a young puppy may feel the need to protect itself from a larger or older dog that may come charging in for a sniff.

It is the guardian's responsibility to protect the puppy so that they do not feel that they must react with fear or aggression in order to protect themselves.

Once your Kangal puppy has received all their vaccinations, you can take them out to public dog parks and various locations where many dogs and people are found.

Before allowing them to interact with other dogs or puppies, take them for a disciplined walk on a leash so that they will be a little tired and less likely to immediately pounce excitedly on all other dogs.

Keep your puppy on a leash and close beside you, because most young puppies are a bundle of out of control energy, and you need to protect them while teaching them how far they can go before they may get themselves into trouble with adult dogs that might not appreciate their excited playfulness.

Remember that they may not have experienced the company of other dogs since you brought them home, and now that they have completed their course of vaccinations, they will understandably be excited and perhaps a little hesitant about seeing dogs again.

Keep a close watch on your Kangal puppy to make sure they are not being overwhelmed by too many other dogs, or getting overly excited and stressed or nervous, because it is your job to protect your puppy.

If your puppy shows any signs of aggression or domination towards another puppy, dog or person, you must immediately step in and calmly discipline them, otherwise by doing nothing, you will be allowing them to get into situations that could become a serious behavioural issues as they grow in age and size.

No matter the age or size of your Kangal puppy, allowing them to display aggression or domination over another dog or person is never a laughing matter and this type of behaviour must be immediately curtailed.

2) With Other People

Take your puppy everywhere with you and introduce them to many different people of all ages, sizes and ethnicities.

This will be easy to do, because most people will automatically be drawn to you when they see you have a puppy because few humans can resist a puppy, especially one as cute as a Kangal.

Most humans will want to interact with your puppy and if they ask to hold your puppy, this is a good opportunity to socialize your puppy and show them that humans are friendly.

Do not let others (especially young children) play roughly with your puppy or squeal at them in a high-pitched voices because this can be very frightening for a sensitive young puppy such as the Kangal.
In addition, you do not want to teach your puppy that humans are a source of crazy, excited energy.

Explain to children that your Kangal puppy is very young and that they must be calm and gentle when playing or interacting in any way.

3) Within Different Environments

It can be a big mistake not to take the time to introduce your Kangal puppy to a wide variety of different environments because when they are not comfortable with different sights and sounds, this could cause them possible trauma later in their adult life.

Be creative and take your puppy everywhere you can imagine when they are young so that no matter where they travel, whether strolling a noisy city sidewalk or along quiet seashore, they will be equally comfortable.

Don't make the mistake of only taking your Kangal puppy into areas where you live and will always travel because they need to also be comfortable visiting areas you might not often visit, such as noisy construction sites, airports or a shopping area across town.

Your puppy needs to see all sorts of sights, sounds and situations so that they will not become fearful should they need to travel with you to any of these areas.

Your Kangal puppy will take their cues from you, which means that when you are calm and in control of every situation, they will learn to be the same because they will trust your lead.
For instance, put your puppy in their Sherpa bag and take them to the airport where they can watch people and hear planes landing and taking off.

Take them to a local park where they can see a baseball game, or take them to the local zoo or farm and let them get a close up look at horses, pigs and ducks.

4) Loud Noises

Many dogs can show extreme fear of loud noises, such as fireworks or thunderstorms.

If you take the time to desensitize your Kangal to these types of noises when they are very young, it will be much easier on them during stormy weather or holidays such as Halloween or New Year's when fireworks are often a part of the festivities.

You can purchase CD's that are a collection of unusual sounds, such as vacuums or hoovers, airplanes, people clapping hands, and more, that you can play while working in your kitchen or relaxing in your living room or lounge.

When you play these sounds and pretend that everything is normal, the next time your puppy or dog hears these types of sounds elsewhere, they will not become upset or agitated because they have learned to ignore them.

Also make sure that you get your young puppy used to the sounds of thunder and fireworks at an early age because these types of shrieking, crashing, banging and popping sounds of fireworks or thunder can be so traumatic and unsettling for many dogs, that sometimes, no matter how much you try to calm your dog, or pretend that everything is fine, there is little you can do.

Some dogs literally lose their minds when they hear the loud popping or screeching noises of fireworks and start running or trying to hide and you cannot communicate with them at all. Make sure that your dog cannot harm itself trying to escape from these types of noises, and if possible, calmly hold them until they begin to relax.

If your dog loses it's mind when it hears these types of noises, simply avoid taking them anywhere near fireworks and if at times when they might hear these noises going off outside, play your inside music or TV louder than you might normally, to help disguise the exterior noise of fireworks or thunder.

Some dogs will respond well to wearing a *"ThunderShirt"* which is specifically designed to alleviate anxiety or trauma associated with loud rumbling, popping or banging noises.

The idea behind the design of the ThunderShirt is that the gentle pressure it creates is similar to a hug that, for some dogs, has a calming effect.

Do not underestimate the importance of taking the time to continually (not just when they are puppies) socialize and desensitize your puppy to all manner of sights, sounds, individuals and locations because to do so will be teaching them to be a calm and well balanced member of your family that will quietly follow you in every situation.

Chapter 9: Training Your Dog

Important note: The Kangal dog can be a good pet IF effectively trained from birth. This truly is very important. If not effectively trained, they can become aggressive dogs.

For most Kangal dogs, the first training centre is their home where other (elder) folks from their kind are present. They develop their guardian instincts by living and learning from the pack.

They socialize with their littermates and learn about their purpose and lifestyle.

So if you are hoping to hone a guardian dog for your livestock, it is best to let the Kangal dog learn from its natural habitat until it is ready to begin performing its duties.

However, most Kangal breeders would not let this happen as the puppy is usually up for adoption from its eighth week. Besides, these puppies are meant to be groomed into companion dogs instead of guardian dogs.

Their training and lifestyle is different from the regular.

1) Intelligent Self-Trainers

Kangal dogs are intelligent self-trainers. They will readily adjust to their home life and respond positively to what is expected of them.

After the first few corrective actions, they will learn to sit when they are commanded to, go outdoors to relieve themselves and follow basic orders to the precise degree. This will make them even more attractive and adorable.

For a moment, you will be misled into believing you've done a real good job training the Kangal dog on your own and that you are going to be fine without formal training sessions.

Kangal dogs are intelligent learners and there is not much you have to do. They will learn gestures and their meaning eagerly.

Although the typical "dog games" might not work out well for the Kangal dog – it will get bored of them sooner than expected – it will not pose many challenges as far as discipline is concerned.

So then does it imply that you do not need to put your Kangal dogs through formal training sessions?

2) Why Is There A Need For Formal Training?

The truth is that Kangal dogs, being guardian dogs, are generally more obedient and attached to their masters. So they will readily learn and act the way you want it to – just to make you happy.

At the same time, do not forget that they own very strong and stubborn personalities.

This implies that when and if there is something that does not agree with them, they will retaliate no matter how adorable they seemed to appear beforehand.

During their puppyhood, they reciprocate the owners' love. But once they hit puberty, they are likely to put their own needs and wants before taking your love into consideration.

This "rebellious" phase becomes more prominent as the Kangal dog approaches puberty.

They will not only exhibit the apparent agitation and interest in other dogs (especially of the opposite gender) but also become overly protective of their possessions – even their food bowls. They will not respond even to the most basic orders and defy all bonds of love and friendship.

So most of those people who decide not to put their Kangal dogs through formal training later end up regretting their decisions.

The importance to beginning training endeavours as early as possible cannot be undermined. As your Kangal puppy grows into a fine dog, its instincts will get reinforced. Their puppyhood is the only time when they can truly be disciplined.

Formal training sessions help owners in establishing their uncontested rule over their pets – at all times. It makes sure your Kangal dog follows your orders regardless of its age. It also helps in keeping its behaviours in control so that other people are safe from it.

These sessions do not only include obedience lessons but also socialization opportunities. So you can take it to places and let it meet with your friends without getting embarrassed.

It is recommended to keep the vaccinations schedule coinciding with your Kangal dog's socialization attempts. It helps in overcoming restlessness and other problems pertaining to agitation.

Your veterinary doctor might be able to suggest some calming solutions to put your pet's nerves at ease.

It is important to keep in mind that socialization and obedience is not exactly normal for the Kangal breed. It will take time and diligence to make sure it understands your motives and complies with them.

In fact, handling the Kangal breed might be a little more difficult than most other dog breeds when it comes to training.

On the same note, remember your Kangal dog does not get fascinated by boring games. So you will need to innovate and create some target-oriented games for your pet.

Give it a mission to fulfil and it will do so. Ask it to fetch a log and it will readily lose interest. Hence the training tactics you use to train the Kangal dog will be very different.

Find and locate dog-training centres in your vicinity. They are a good source of information and advice. You can have your pet enrolled in one of these.

Ask other people from your neighbourhood who are in possession of a dog about where and how they trained their canine companions.

The needs of every dog are different, so if you are a first time owner of the Kangal dog, you will need all the help and information you can get from other sources.

It is a tough dog, so you need to be tougher to show it who sets the rules and who follows them.

3) Trainability

As the Kangal has two relatively intelligent parents, they will almost undoubtedly also be an intelligent and fairly easy to train dog.

When taught with positive reinforcement, they will be eager learners who will easily excel at anything you have the time and patience to teach.

No matter what you decide to teach your Kangal, always train with patience and kindness and NEVER yell, hit or punish a dog during training, or at any time for that matter.

Using harsh, mean or loud training methods could frighten a Kangal and cause them to shut down. Any sort of harsh treatment will cause your friendly and sensitive Kangal to lose trust and respect of you, and they could also learn to fear you, which is NOT the type of relationship you want to have with your dog.

All training sessions should be happy and fun filled with plenty of rewards and positive reinforcement, which will ensure that your Kangal is an excellent student who looks forward to learning new commands and tricks.

The Kangal can be very skilful in many different forms of advanced dog sports, including agility, obedience, freestyle dance, rally, and more.

4) Puppy Training Basics

Most humans believe that they need to take their young dog to puppy classes, and generally speaking, this is a good idea for any young Kangal (after they have had their vaccinations), because it will help to get them socialized.

Beyond puppy classes for socialization reasons, hiring a professional dog whisperer for personalized private sessions to train the humans may be far more valuable than training situations where there are multiple dogs and humans together in one class as this can be very distracting for everyone concerned.

a. Three Most Important Words

"Come", **"Sit"** and **"Stay"** will be the three most important words you will ever teach your Kangal puppy.

These three basic commands will ensure that your Kangal remains safe in almost every circumstance.

For instance, when your puppy correctly learns the "Come" command, you can always quickly bring them back to your side if you should see danger approaching.

When you teach your Kangal puppy the "Sit" and "Stay" commands you will be further establishing your leadership role. A puppy that understands that their human guardian is their leader will be a safe and happy follower.

b. Choosing a Discipline Sound

Choosing a *"discipline sound"* that will be the same for every human family member will make it much easier for your puppy to learn what they can or cannot do and will be very useful when warning your Kangal puppy before they engage in unwanted behaviour.

The best types of sounds are short and sharp so that you and your family members can quickly say them and so that the sound will immediately get the attention of your Kangal puppy because you want to be able to easily interrupt them when they are about to make a mistake.

It doesn't really matter what the sound is, so long as everyone in the family is consistent.

A sound that is very effective for most puppies and dogs is a simple ***"UH"*** sound said sharply and with emphasis.

Most puppies and dogs respond immediately to this sound and if caught in the middle of doing something they are not supposed to be doing will quickly stop and give you their attention or back away from what they were doing.

5) Beginner Leash Lesson

Equipment: 4 or 6-foot leash and Martingale training collar.

The most important ongoing bonding exercise you will experience with your new Kangal puppy is when you go out for your daily walks together.

Far, far too many people ignore this critical, multi-tasking time that is not only important for your puppy's exercise, but also fulfils a multitude of their needs, including:

- Exercising their body
- Fulfilling their natural roaming urges
- Teaching them discipline, which engages their mind
- Learning to follow, trust and respect you

As soon as you bring your new puppy home you will want to teach them how to walk at your side while on leash without pulling.

Every time your puppy needs to go out to relieve his or herself, slip on their collar and snap on the leash.

At first your Kangal puppy may struggle or fight against having a collar around their neck, because the sensation will be new to them. However, at the same time they will want to go with you, so exercise patience and encourage them to walk with you.

Be careful never to drag them, and if they pull backwards and refuse to walk forwards with you, simply stop for a moment, while keeping slight forward tension on the leash, until your Kangal puppy gives up and moves forward. Immediately reward them with your happy praise, and if they have a favourite treat, this can be an added incentive when teaching them to walk on their leash.

Always walk your puppy on your left side with the leash slack so that they learn that walking with you is a relaxing experience. Keep the leash short enough so that they do not have enough slack to get in front of you.

If they begin to create tension in the leash by pulling forward or to the side, simply stop moving, get them back beside you, and start over.

Be patient and consistent with your puppy and very soon they will understand exactly where their walking position is and will walk easily beside you without any pulling or leash tension.

Remember that walking with a new puppy is an exciting experience for them as they will want to sniff everything and explore their new world, so give them lots of understanding and don't expect them to be perfect all the time.

When your Kangal puppy is very young, and wanting to put everything in their mouths, walk them in a harness and collar and leash, so that you can have a second leash attached to the harness.

This way, you will be able to easily lift them over cigarette butts or other garbage you may encounter while out walking. Once they grow out of the habit of tasting all manner of garbage, you can dispense with the harness and second leash.

6) Surviving Adolescence

The adolescent period in a young Kangal's life, between the ages of 6 and 12 months, is the transitional stage of both physical and psychological development when they are physically almost fully-grown in size, yet their minds are still developing and they are testing their boundaries and the limits that their human counterparts will endure.

This can be a dangerous time in a puppy's life because this is when they start to make decisions on their own which, if they do not receive the leadership they need from their human guardians, can lead to developing unwanted behaviour.

Learning how to make decisions on their own would be perfectly normal and desirable if your Kangal puppy was living in the wild, amongst a pack of dogs, because learning to make decisions would be necessary for their survival.

However, when living within a human environment, your puppy must always adhere to human rules and it will be up to their human guardians to continue their vigilant, watchful guidance in order to make sure that they do.

Many humans are lulled into a false sense of security when their new Kangal puppy reaches the age of approximately six months, because the puppy has been well socialized, they have been to puppy classes and long since been house trained.

The real truth is that the serious work is only now beginning and the humans and their new Kangal puppy could be in for a time of testing that could seriously challenge the relationship and leave the humans wondering if they made the right decision to share their home with a dog.

If the human side of the relationship is not prepared for this transitional time in their young dog's life, their patience may be seriously tried, and the relationship of trust and respect that has been previously built can be damaged, and could take considerable time to repair.
While not all adolescent puppies will experience a noticeable adolescent period of craziness, because every puppy is different, most young dogs do commonly exhibit at least some of the usual adolescent behaviours, including reverting to previous puppy behaviours.

Some of these adolescent behaviours might include destructive chewing of objects they have previously shown no interest in, selective hearing or ignoring previously learned commands, displaying aggressive behaviour, jumping on everyone, barking at everything that moves, or reverting to relieving themselves in the house, even though they were house trained months ago.

Keeping your cool and recognizing these adolescent signs is the first step towards helping to make this transition period easier on your Kangal puppy and all family members.

The first step to take that can help keep raging hormones at bay is to spay or neuter your Kangal puppy just prior to the onset of adolescence, at around four or five months of age.

While spaying or neutering a Kangal puppy will not entirely eliminate the adolescent phase, it will certainly help and at the same time will spare your puppy the added strain of both the physical and emotional changes that occur during sexual maturity.

As well, some female puppies will become extremely aggressive towards other dogs during heat, and non-neutered males may become territorially aggressive and pick fights with other males.

Once your Kangal puppy has been spayed or neutered, you will want to become more active with your young dog, both mentally and physically by providing them with continued and more complex disciplined exercises.

This can be accomplished by enrolling your adolescent Kangal in a dog whispering session or more advanced training class, which will help them to continue their socialization skills while also developing their brain.

Even though it may be more difficult to train during this period, having the assistance of a professional and continuing the experience of ongoing socialization amongst other dogs of a similar size can be invaluable, as this is the time when many young dogs begin to show signs of antisocial behaviour with other dogs as well as unknown humans.

When your Kangal is provided with sufficient daily exercise and continued socialization with unfamiliar dogs, people and places that provide interest and expand their mind, they will be able to transition through the adolescent stage of their life much more seamlessly.

7) Releasing Energy

The adolescent period in a puppy's life is a time of boundless energy and you will need to find ways to safely allow them to release this energy every day. Since most humans cannot walk nearly fast enough to accommodate the needs of an energetic puppy, you will first want to walk your Kangal beside you on a leash, and then find a safe place where they can run off the leash, either chasing a ball, retrieving a Frisbee or playing and running in an enclosed area with other similar sized dogs where you can always supervise them.

8) The Unruly Adolescent

If your Kangal puppy happens to be especially unruly during their adolescent phase, you will need to simply limit their opportunities for making mistakes.
For instance, a puppy who is digging up the yard, or chewing up just about anything they can get their teeth into will need to be closely supervised so that you can direct their energy into less harmful pursuits.

It does absolutely no good to yell at your Kangal puppy for engaging in behaviour you are not happy with, and in fact, yelling or getting angry will only desensitize your young dog from listening to any of your commands.

Furthermore, although you may eventually get the results you want, if you yell loud enough, your puppy will then be reacting out of fear, rather than respect, and this will be damaging to your relationship.

Displaying calm, yet assertive energy is the only energy that works well to help your adolescent puppy understand what is required of them.

All other human emotions (frustration, anger, impatience, sadness, excitement) are "read" by puppies and dogs as being unstable, and not only will the smart and sensitive Kangal not understand these emotions, they will not respect you for displaying these types of unstable energies.

An extremely rambunctious adolescent Kangal may need to have their free run of the house curtailed so that they are confined to areas where you can easily supervise them.

Make sure they are within eyesight at all times, so that if they do find an opportunity to make a mistake, you can quickly show them what is permitted and what is not.
Adolescence may also be a time when you might have to insist that your young Kangal sleeps in their crate with the door closed whenever you cannot supervise, as well as at bedtime so they continue to understand that you have firm rules.

Keeping on top of house training is also a good idea during the adolescent period of your puppy's life because some adolescent puppies may become stubborn and forget that they are already house trained.

This means actually taking the time to be involved in the process by leashing up your Kangal and physically taking them outside whenever they need to relieve themselves. This sort of a routine is also a disciplined exercise that will help to reinforce in your puppy's mind that you are the boss.

Too many humans with convenient yards simply do not participate at all in the bathroom routine of their young dogs and thereby miss out on endless opportunities to reinforce who is the boss.

9) Rewarding Unwanted Behaviour

Often humans make the mistake of accidentally rewarding unwanted behaviour.

It is very important to recognize that any attention paid to an overly excited, out of control, adolescent puppy, even negative attention, is likely going to be rewarding for your puppy.

Therefore, when you engage with an out of control Kangal puppy, you end up actually rewarding them, which will encourage them to continue more of this unwanted behaviour.

Be aware that chasing after a puppy when they have taken something they are not supposed to have, picking them up when they are barking or showing aggression, pushing them off when they jump on you or other people, or yelling when they refuse to come when called, are all forms of attention that can actually be rewarding for most puppies.

As your Kangal's guardian, it will be your responsibility to provide calm and consistent structure for your puppy, which will include finding acceptable and safe ways to allow your puppy to vent their energy without being destructive or harmful to property, other dogs, humans, or the actual puppy.

Activities that create or encourage an overly excited Kangal puppy, such as rough games of tug-o-war, or wild games of chase through the living room, should be immediately curtailed, so that your adolescent puppy learns how to control their energy and play quietly and appropriately without jumping on everyone or engaging in barking or mouthy behaviour.

Furthermore, if your adolescent Kangal puppy displays excited energy simply from being petted by you, your family members or any visitors, you will need to teach yourself, your family and your friends to ignore your puppy until they calm down. Otherwise, you will be teaching your Kangal puppy that the touch of humans means excitement.

Once your puppy has learned that humans are a source of excitement, you will then have to work very long and hard to reverse this behaviour.

Children are often a source of excitement that can cause an adolescent puppy to be extremely wound up.

Do not allow your children to engage with an adolescent Kangal puppy unless you are there to supervise and teach the children appropriate and calm ways to interact with the puppy.
In order to keep everyone safe, it is very important that your Kangal puppy learn at an early age that neither children nor adults are sources of excitement.

You can help develop the mind of an adolescent Kangal and the minds of growing children at the same time by teaching children that your puppy needs structured walks and by showing them how to play fetch, search, hide and seek, or how to teach the Kangal puppy simple tricks and obedience skills that will be a fun and positive interaction for everyone.

10) Back to Basics

When your puppy is going through what could be a belligerent and trying adolescence, when it seems that they have forgotten everything they may have learned so far, this is an especially good time to revisit the simple "Sit" command.

Now, in order to help re-establish your leadership role, you will want to ask your Kangal puppy to sit at every opportunity.

The simple act of "sitting" will help to calm an excited mind and will get your puppy's focus back on you.

11) Sit and More Sit

Every time you take your Kangal out for a walk, which is usually a cause of excitement, get into the habit of asking them to sit while you put on their leash — then ask them to sit and calmly wait while you put on your shoes or jacket — after you approach the door, ask them to sit again while you open the door — after you are on the other side of the door — ask them to sit again while you lock the door.

If there are stairs or landings involved, ask them to sit at the top and also again at the bottom.

Every time you arrive at street intersections or a crossing, ask your Kangal puppy to sit again, and do this in reverse when coming back home.

Every time you stop during your walk to speak to a neighbour, greet a friend or admire the view, ask your puppy to sit.

Every time you ask your young dog to sit for you, they are learning several things all at once — that they must remain calm, that you are the boss and that they must respect you as their leader.

In addition, a sitting puppy is much easier to control than one standing alert, ready to bolt out the door or jump on someone.

Once your puppy is reliably sitting for you at least 50% of the time with voice command, also include the hand signal for "Sit", so that they will hear the word and also see the signal.

While you can use any hand signal, the universal hand signal for "Sit" is:

Right arm (palm open facing upward) parallel to the floor, and then raising your arm, while bent at the elbow toward your right shoulder.

Once your Kangal is sitting reliable for you, remove the verbal "Sit" and replace it with the hand signal.

It's important to begin teaching hand signals during the adolescent stage of your puppy's life, because this will also help them to communicate in a way that is more natural for a dog —

by watching you and feeling your energy, rather than always having to hear you speak a command.

As well, because the action of sitting helps to calm the mind of an excited puppy (or dog), teaching your puppy the “Sit” command is a very important part of their daily interactions with your family members as well as people you may meet when out on a walk.

When you ask your puppy to "Sit" before you interact in any way with them, before you go out or in every door, before you feed them, etc., you are helping to quiet their mind, while making it more difficult for them to jump, lunge or disappear out a door.

The adolescent stage in a young dog’s life is the perfect time to begin teaching hand signals for all your common commands, because they must look at you to understand what is expected of them, and when they are looking at you, they are more focused and less likely to take matters into their own paws.

12) Giving Up is Not an Option

Too often we humans get frustrated and give up on our dogs when they change from being the cute, cuddly and mostly obedient little puppy they once were, and become all kinds of trouble you never bargained for, as they grow into their adolescent stage.

It will be during the confusing adolescent stage of a dog’s life that they find themselves abandoned and behind bars as their humans who promised to love and protect them leave their once loved fur friend at the local pound or SPCA.

First of all, not all dogs go through a crazy adolescent period, and secondly, even if they do, please read this section carefully, because you can live through puppy adolescence and come out the other side relatively unscathed and a much more knowledgeable and patient guardian.

Congratulations are in order because you've been successful with potty training your young Kangal puppy and with teaching them to sleep in their own kennel at night.

Furthermore, you've lived through the teething troubles, the chewing and the hand nipping and you no longer have to get up at 3:00 a.m. to let your puppy out to relieve itself.

In addition, you've taught your Kangal puppy their first few basic commands, and socialized them with many other dogs, people and places, so you should feel proud of all your accomplishments and the leaps and bounds you and your puppy have accomplished together over the last several months.

Even though your adolescent puppy may be starting to act like a Tasmanian devil, and you may be having second thoughts, now is not the time to give up on them and yourself just because it may seem like someone switched your dog when you weren't looking.

Now is the time to remain calmly consistent and persistent, and to know that you will eventually be able to enjoy the happy rewards of your entire puppy raising diligence.

Of course, this dramatic switch from being the world's best puppy into the monster you can no longer control is not true for all puppies, as every puppy is unique.

However, being prepared for the worst will help you ride any impending storm and get you both out the other side where you can enjoy an even closer relationship than you previously had.

If you are at the stage with your puppy that you are having great difficulties and wondering if you made the right decision to share your home with a dog, rest assured that puppy adolescence is a normal phase of their development, which can be managed, and which will definitely pass.

As well, if you are finding yourself totally overwhelmed, there are many professionals who can provide valuable assistance to help you through this stage of your Kangal puppy's development.

For most puppies, adolescence will begin between the ages of five and seven months and this is also the time that you need to be making an appointment at your veterinarian's office to have your puppy spayed or neutered.

Although neutering or spaying will not prevent adolescent behaviour entirely, it can certainly reduce the intensity of it, as during this period there are hormonal changes occurring that will affect your puppy's behaviour.

While it's usually hormones that are the major cause of behavioural changes in your adolescent puppy, there are also physical changes occurring at the same time that you may not be aware of.

For instance, your puppy will be going through physical growth spurts which might be causing them some pain, as well as changes related to growth in their brain while your puppy's cerebral cortex becomes more involved in thinking for itself.

Usually, during this time of brain growth, a puppy will be trying to make choices for themselves, and may or may not yet be capable of making the right choices. This is why their behaviour can appear to be quite erratic.

During the early adolescent period of brain development in your Kangal puppy, the signals sometimes get mixed up and rerouted, which can result in the perplexing responses you might notice, when for instance, you ask you puppy to sit and they stare dumbly at you, even though they learned this command months ago.

Don't worry because your previous training will return.

13) Hand Signals

Hand signal training is by far the most useful and efficient training method for every dog, including the Kangal.

This is because all too often we inundate our canine companions with a great deal of chatter and noise that they really do not understand because English is not their first language.

Contrary to what some humans might think, the first language of a Kangal, or any dog, is a combination of sensing energy and watching body language, which requires no spoken word or sound.

Therefore, when we humans take the time to teach our dog hand signals for all their basic commands, we are communicating with them at a level they instinctively understand, plus we are helping them to become a focused follower, as they must watch us to understand what is required of them.

If you teach your dog hand signals from the start, it will be much easier for you and your dog when he becomes a senior and his hearing might be affected. That way, should he become deaf, you can still communicate with your dog.

a. Come

Come: you can kneel down for this command or stay standing. Open your arms wide like you are hugging a very large tree. This hand signal can be seen from a long distance.

When first teaching hand signals to your Kangal, always show the hand signal for the command at the same time you say the word.

If they are totally ignoring the command, it will be time to incorporate a lunge line, which is a very long leash to help you teach the "Come" command.

Simply attach a 20-foot line to their collar and let them sniff about in a large yard or at your neighbourhood park.

If they still do not "Come" toward you, simply reel them in until they are in front of you. Then let them wander about again, until you are ready to ask them to "Come".

Repeat this process until your Kangal responds correctly at least 80% of the time. You can also reinforce the command by giving a treat when they come back to you when asked. Always ask them to "Sit" when they return to you.

b. Sit

Sit: right arm (palm open facing upward) parallel to the floor, and then raise your arm, while bent at the elbow toward your shoulder.

Sit is a very simple, yet extremely valuable command for all puppies and dogs.

If your dog is not sitting on command, try holding a treat above and slightly behind their head, so that when they look up for it they may automatically sit to see it.

Slowly remove the treats as reward and replace the treat with a "life reward", such as a chest rub or a scratch behind the ears and your happy smile.

If your Kangal is not particularly treat motivated, lift up and slightly back on the leash when asking them to sit (stand in front of them), and if they still are having difficulties, reach down with your free hand, place it across your dog's back at the place where the back legs join the hip and gently squeeze.

Remember - Do NOT simply push down on your dog's back to force their hind legs to collapse under them as this pressure could harm their spine or leg joints.

c. Stay

Stay: right arm fully extended towards your dog's head, palm open, hand bent up at the wrist.

Once your Kangal is in the "Sit" position, ask them to "Stay" with both the verbal cue and the hand signal.

TIP: if you are right-handed, use your right arm and hand for the signal, and if you are left-handed, use your left arm and hand for the signal. Using your dominant hand will be much more effective because your strongest energy emanates from the palm of your dominant hand.

While your dog is sitting and staying, slowly back away from them. If they move from their position, calmly put them back into Sit and ask them to "Stay" again, using both the verbal cue and the hand signal.

Continue to practice this until your dog understands that you want them to stay sitting and not move towards you.

With all commands, when your Kangal is just learning, be patient and always reward them with a treat and your happy praise for a job well done.

14) Simple Tricks

When teaching your Kangal tricks, in order to give them extra incentive, find a treat that they really like, and give the treat as rewards and to help solidify a good performance.

Most dogs will be extra attentive during training sessions when they know that they will be rewarded with their favourite treats.

If your Kangal is less than six months old when you begin teaching them tricks, keep your training sessions short (no more than 5 or 10 minutes) and fun, and as they become adults, you can extend your sessions as they will be able to maintain their focus for longer periods of time.

a. Shake a Paw

Who doesn't love a dog that knows how to shake a paw? This is one of the easiest tricks to teach your Kangal.

TIP: most dogs are naturally either right or left pawed. If you know which paw your dog favours, ask them to shake this paw.

Find a quiet place to practice, without noisy distractions or other pets, and stand or sit in front of your dog. Place them in the sitting position and have a treat in your left hand.

Say the command *"Shake"* while putting your right hand behind their left or right paw and pulling the paw gently toward yourself until you are holding their paw in your hand. Immediately praise them and give them the treat.

Most dogs will learn the "Shake" trick very quickly, and very soon, once you put out your hand, your Kangal will immediately lift their paw and put it into your hand, without your assistance or any verbal cue.

Practice every day until they are 100% reliable with this trick, and then it will be time to add another trick to their repertoire.

b. Roll Over

You will find that just like your Kangal is naturally either right or left pawed, that they will also naturally want to roll either to the right or the left side. Take advantage of this by asking your dog to roll to the side they naturally prefer.

Sit with your dog on the floor and put them in a lie down position. Hold a treat in your hand and place it close to their nose without allowing them to grab it, and while they are in the lying position, move the treat to the right or left side of their head so that they have to roll over to get to it.

You will very quickly see which side they want to naturally roll to, and once you see this, move the treat to this side. Once they roll over to this side, immediately give them the treat and praise them.

You can say the verbal cue *"Over"* while you demonstrate the hand signal motion (moving your right hand in a circular motion) or moving the treat from one side of their head to the other with a half circle motion.

15) Adult Training

The Kangal is an intelligent breed that will be skilful in many different dog sports, such as agility, obedience, or freestyle dance.

When your Kangal is a fully-grown adult (approximately two years of age), you will definitely want to begin more complicated or advanced training sessions.

They will enjoy it and when you have the desire and patience, there is no end to the tricks or routines you can teach a willing Kangal.

For instance, you may wish to teach your adult Kangal more advanced tricks, such as how to dance, or the opposite sided paw shakes or rollovers, which are more difficult than you might expect.

If you and your Kangal are really enjoying learning new tricks together, you might want to advance to teaching them the *"commando crawl"*, how to *"speak"* or to *"jump through the human hoop"*.

All of these tricks and many more are fun to teach and will exercise both your Kangal's mind and body by taking advantage of their natural ability to excel as an entertaining circus performer.

The more control you have over your Kangal, the easier it will be to teach them a fun sport, such as Agility or Freestyle dance.

The only restriction to how far you can go with training your adult Kangal will be your imagination and their personal ability or desire to perform.

16) Behavioural Issues

It can be difficult, if not impossible to generalize or speculate with respect to alleviating possible behavioural issues or problems because, in most cases, a dog suffering from behavioural issues requires the assistance of a dog whisperer or dog psychologist.

When reading anything about how to prevent or cure behavioural issues, please be aware that behavioural problems most often cannot be properly assessed or cured by reading a book.

The reason for this is because there are just too many variables and unique situations, individual dogs, individual humans, unique circumstances, and endless reasons why they may have developed any particular behavioural issue.

Therefore, without knowing the dog's particulars and all the history of what has transpired between the Kangal and their guardian that came before, attempting to write about how to cure a particular issue will be no more than a best guess.

This is why someone whose dog is suffering from a specific behavioural issue that is in turn, at the least embarrassing, or at the worst, driving the humans and the entire neighbourhood crazy, must be properly addressed by engaging the services of a professional dog whisperer (psychologist or behaviourist) who can ask many questions, properly assess the situation and then design a unique plan for alleviating the problem.

17) Overheating

Be very careful that you do not allow them to become overheated when training or walking your Kangal outside during hot weather. Always carry water with you to help keep them hydrated.

TIP: if your Kangal has a coat that is darker colored, you can easily help to keep them cooler on hot, sunny days by having them wear a light-weight vest that is a lighter colour than their own coat.

Remember that they are close to heated pavement or road surface, which means that on a hot, sunny day, they will literally be heated from both the bottom and the top.

If the pavement is very hot, do not allow them to walk on it. Instead, take them to a grassy area for their exercise.

Chapter 10: Poisonous Foods & Plants

As much as you love your Kangal pet, the last thing you want will be to poison it either knowingly or unknowingly. Here are some of the things you need to be careful about while handling and caring for your Kangal dog.

1) Popular Poisoning Agents

Similar to human foods, human medicines can cause poisoning in Kangal dogs. Make sure you keep the medicine cabinet shut tightly at all times.

Keep medicines out of reach of naïve beings – whether it is children or animals. If you suspect there is a breach, consult the emergency services immediately.

A common example is ibuprofen – a single dose can cause stomach ulcers in Kangal dogs.

Besides this, all kinds of chemicals can prove to be lethal for your pet. So whether it is the pesticide you used on your lawn, the cleaner you used to remove that stubborn stain on your carpet or an accidental leakage of fluids from your car – keep your Kangal dog away from the crime site.

Licking these hazardous liquids can cause a wide assortment of problems ranging from minor upset stomach to poisoning and death.

Do not give your Kangal dog a lot of home food, as its digestive tract is not meant for such items. Use high quality dog foods only.

Moreover, do not give it any food that contains chocolates, tea, coffee, onions, garlic or other similar items (mentioned previously). Its diet is imperative to its health so make these decisions wisely.

On the same note, avoid giving any medicines to your Kangal dog until and unless specified by a certified veterinary doctor. You never know when a chemical composition may backfire and aggravate your pet's health.

The veterinarian knows best and hence these matters should be left at their discretion alone.

In case you suspect your Kangal dog has ingested some kind of a chemical (or you know it has), rush it to the veterinary doctor immediately. If there are any poison control centres in your vicinity, take your pet there immediately.

These facilities will identify the type of chemical ingested and will immediately try to neutralize its effects. Do not wait and see what happens (or what does not happen) as you may exacerbate the situation before your dog is able to receive medical help.

Use safety latches everywhere to store toxic and potentially lethal concoctions. If there is still a breach, consult the experts immediately.

When it comes to the Kangal dog, ingestion is not the only way it can be poisoned. Its natural curiosity to sniff at different objects and then try to taste them can also lead to poisoning.

The most common way this can happen inside your home is when your dog goes near toxic plants.

Plants such as aloe vera, hyacinth, yew, elephant's ear and several others are known to contain chemicals that are not tolerated well by most dogs.

Consequently, when they try experimenting with these plants (whether indoors or outdoors), the chances of poisoning become elevated.

It is best to keep these plants behind barriers of some kind to ensure your dog does not come into contact with them. Moreover, if there are any signs of a breach, rush your pet in for medical care immediately.

Once you have an idea about the items that can poison your beloved canine companion, the next most important thing for you to know is what symptoms your pet will exhibit in case it is poisoned.

Read through the next section carefully to find out how to spot a poisoned Kangal dog.

2) Common Symptoms of Poisoning

It is impossible to keep guard over your pet at all times. Naturally, it opens a window of opportunity for your pet to explore around your place. When it is on this mission, it seldom will respect the boundaries you set for your pet.

On its exploration spree, it can come into contact with or try to ingest those items that can cause poisoning.

Here are some of the symptoms you should look out for that point towards the possibility of poisoning. So even if you were not on guard, you can save your pet from an unfortunate fate by rushing it to the vet in time.

1. Abdominal pain.
Your dog will suddenly begin to whine a lot and when you try to touch its abdomen you will feel it has become tender.

2. Coma.
Your canine friend will refuse to respond to your orders and will remain in a subconscious state for extended periods of time.
At this time, you should absolutely take no time to get it to a veterinary doctor as this symbolizes an aggravated stage of poisoning.

3. Convulsions.
Poison can trigger convulsions in your pet.
Rush it to the vet immediately if your pet begins to convulse all of a sudden.

5. Diarrhoea.
Poisons will disrupt its digestive system. So if you see unexplained loose stools, rush to the poison control centre or vet immediately.
Admittedly, this is a much "lighter" version of poisoning. Nevertheless, untimely help can lead it to a horrific fate.

6. Drooling.
It is not much of a problem as most Kangal dogs are likely to drool. It is normal for quite a few.
However, if you observe your Kangal dog has suddenly started drooling even though it did not do so before, consult a vet.

7. Irregular heartbeat.
Placing a hand on its chest will tell you if its heartbeat is normal or not.
Like humans, the heartbeats are quite superficial. If you see your Kangal dog exhibiting some of the aforementioned characteristics, immediately roll it over and feel for its heartbeat. If it is irregular, you know what you need to do.

8. Difficulty breathing.
It will become evident to you when and if your pet is facing difficulty breathing. It will be making a conscious effort to keep

breathing and will refuse to perform any strenuous activities. This will become even more evident if you observe it closely for a few minutes while it is lying on the floor.

9. Fatigue.
If your canine companion feels tired, it will automatically show on its face.
Just keep a close eye on the signs it is giving off and those that are normal to it. Any deviation is almost always an indicator of trouble.

10. Swollen limbs.
Toxins in poisons can cause swelling in its limbs as well as in its internal organs. If it becomes apparent on its limbs, rush it to the emergency services immediately.
You never know if internal swelling, for example on its windpipe, might become a major threat to its survival.

11. Vomiting.
Anything that is not tolerated well by its body is likely to be expelled in the form of vomit.
However, this does not happen every time it tries to ingest poison. If you are sure there is absolutely no other reason why your pet should begin vomiting all of a sudden, rush it to the vet immediately.

If you observe any or all of these symptoms in your pet and you know that they are not normal, consult a veterinarian immediately.

If it is too difficult to seek out a veterinarian, look for the nearest poison control centre for dogs. In such a situation, time is extremely sensitive to your pet's health. So don't procrastinate and don't take any chances.

Your pet deserves the best so make sure you don't let it down on this.

3) Poisonous Foods

While some dogs are smart enough not to want to eat foods that can harm or kill them, other canine companions will eat absolutely anything they can get their teeth into.

As conscientious guardians for our furry friends, it will always be our responsibility to make certain that when we share our homes with a dog, we never leave foods that could be toxic or lethal to them easily within their reach.

While there are many foods that can be toxic to a Kangal, the following alphabetical list contains some of the more common foods that can seriously harm or even kill our dogs including:

Bread Dough: if your dog eats bread dough, their body heat will cause the dough to rise inside the stomach. As the dough expands during the rising process, alcohol is produced.

Dogs who have eaten bread dough may experience stomach bloating, abdominal pain, vomiting, disorientation and depression. Because bread dough can rise to many times its original size, eating only a small amount will cause a problem for any dog.

Broccoli: the toxic ingredient in broccoli is isothiocynate. While it may cause stomach upset, it probably won't be very harmful unless the amount eaten is more than 10% of the dog's total daily diet.

Chocolate: contains theobromine, a chemical that is toxic to dogs in large enough quantities. Chocolate also contains caffeine, which is found in coffee, tea, and certain soft drinks. Different types of chocolate contain different amounts of theobromine and caffeine.

For example, dark chocolate and baking chocolate or cocoa powder contain more of these compounds than milk chocolate does, therefore, a dog would need to eat more milk chocolate in order to become ill.

However, even a few ounces of chocolate can be enough to cause illness or death in a puppy, therefore no amount or type of chocolate should be considered safe for a dog to eat.

Chocolate toxicity can cause vomiting, diarrhoea, rapid or irregular heart rate, restlessness, muscle tremors and seizures. Death can occur within 24 hours of eating.

During many holidays such as Christmas, New Year's, Valentine's, Easter and Halloween, chocolate is often more easily accessible to curious dogs, especially from children who are not so careful with where they might keep their Halloween or Easter egg stash and who are an easy mark for a hungry dog.

In some cases, people unwittingly poison their dogs by offering them chocolate as a treat or leaving chocolate cookies or frosted cake easily within licking distance.

Caffeine: beverages containing caffeine, such as soda, tea, coffee, and chocolate, act as a stimulant and can accelerate your dog's heartbeat to a dangerous level. Dogs eating caffeine have been known to have seizures, some of which are fatal.

Cooked Bones: can be extremely hazardous for a dog because the bones become brittle when cooked, which causes them to splinter when the dog chews on them.

The splinters have sharp edges that have been known to become stuck in the teeth, and cause choking when caught in the throat or create a rupture or puncture of the stomach lining or intestinal tract.

Especially dangerous are cooked turkey and chicken legs, ham, pork chop and veal bones. Symptoms of choking include:

- Pale or blue gums
- Gasping open-mouthed breathing
- Pawing at the face
- Slow, shallow breathing
- Falling unconscious with dilated pupils

Grapes and Raisins: can cause acute (sudden) kidney failure in dogs. While it is not known what the toxic agent is in this fruit, clinical signs can occur within 24 hours of eating and include vomiting, diarrhoea, and lethargy (tiredness).

Other signs of illness caused from eating grapes or raisins relate to the eventual shutdown of kidney functioning.

Garlic and Onions: contain chemicals that damage red blood cells by rupturing them so that they lose their ability to carry oxygen effectively, which leave the dog short of oxygen, causing what is called *"hemolytic anaemia"*.

Poisoning can occur with a single ingestion of large quantities of garlic or onions or with repeated meals containing small amounts.

Cooking does not reduce the potential toxicity of onions and garlic.

NOTE: fresh, cooked, and/or powdered garlic or onions are commonly found in baby food, which is sometimes given to dogs when they are sick, therefore, be certain to carefully read food labels before feeding to your Kangal.

Macadamia Nuts: are commonly found in candies and chocolates. Although the mechanism of macadamia nut toxicity is not well understood, the clinical signs in dogs having eaten these nuts include depression, weakness, vomiting, tremors, joint pain, and pale gums.
Signs can occur within 12 hours after eating. In some cases, symptoms can resolve themselves without treatment within 24 to 48 hours; however, keeping a close eye on your Kangal will be strongly recommended.

Mushrooms: mushroom poisoning can be fatal if certain species of mushrooms are eaten.

The most commonly reported severely toxic species of mushroom in the US is Amanita phalloides (Death Cap mushroom), which is also quite a common species found in most parts of Britain. Other Amanita species are also toxic.

This deadly mushroom is often found growing in grassy or wooded areas near various deciduous and coniferous trees, which mean that if you're out walking with your Kangal in the woods, they could easily find these mushrooms.

Eating them can cause severe liver disease and neurological disorders. If you suspect your dog has eaten these mushrooms, immediately take them to your veterinarian, as the recommended treatment is to induce vomiting and to give activated charcoal. Further treatment for liver disease may also be necessary.

Pits and Seeds: many seeds and pits found in a variety of fruits, including apples, apricots, cherries, pears and plums, contain cyanogenic glycosides that can cause cyanide poisoning in your Kangal.

The symptoms of cyanide poisoning usually occur within 15-20 minutes to a few hours after eating and symptoms can include initial excitement, followed by rapid respiration rate, salivation, voiding of urine and faeces, vomiting, muscle spasm, staggering, and coma before death.

Dogs suffering from cyanide poisoning that live more than 2 hours after onset of symptoms will usually recover.

Raw Salmon or Trout: Salmon Poisoning Disease (SPD) can be a problem for anyone who goes fishing with their dog, or feeds their dog a raw meat diet that includes raw salmon or trout.

When a snail is infected and then is eaten by the fish, as part of the food chain, the dog is exposed when it eats the infected fish.

A sudden onset of symptoms can occur 5-7 days after eating the infected fish. In the acute stages, gastrointestinal symptoms are quite similar to canine parvovirus.

SPD has a mortality rate of up to 90%, can be diagnosed with a faecal sample and is treatable if caught on time.

Prevention is simple, cook all fish before feeding it to your Kangal and immediately see your veterinarian if you suspect that your dog has eaten raw salmon or trout.

Tobacco: all forms of tobacco, including patches, nicotine gum and chewing tobacco can be fatal to dogs if eaten.

Signs of poisoning can appear within an hour and include hyperactivity, salivation, panting, vomiting and diarrhoea. Advanced signs include muscle weakness, twitching, collapse, coma, increased heart rate and eventually cardiac arrest.

Never leave tobacco products within reach of your dog, and be careful not to let them pick up discarded cigarette butts when they are young puppies.

If you suspect your dog has eaten any of these, seek immediate veterinary help.

TIP: when your Kangal is a very young puppy, use a double leash, collar and harness arrangement, so that you can still teach them to walk on a leash with a Martingale collar around their neck, but can also attach the second leash to their harness so that you can easily lift them over enticing cigarette butts or other toxic garbage they may be trying to eat during your walks.

Tomatoes: contain atropine, which can cause dilated pupils, tremors and irregular heartbeat. The highest concentration of atropine is found in the leaves and stems of tomato plants, next is the unripe (green) tomatoes, followed by the ripe tomato.

Xylitol: is an artificial sweetener found in products such as gum, candy, mints, toothpaste, and mouthwash that is recognized by the National Animal Poison Control Centre to be a risk to dogs.

Xylitol is harmful to dogs because it causes a sudden release of insulin in the body that leads to hypoglycaemia (low blood sugar). Xylitol can also cause liver damage in dogs.

Within 30 minutes after eating a product containing xylitol, the dog may vomit, be lethargic (tired), and/or be uncoordinated. However, some signs of toxicity can also be delayed for hours or even for a few days. Xylitol toxicity in dogs can be fatal if left untreated.

Please be aware that the above list is just some of the more common foods that can be toxic or fatal to our fur friends and that there are many other foods we should never be feeding our dogs.

If you have one of those dogs who will happily eat anything that looks or smells even slightly like food, be certain to keep these foods far away from your beloved dog and you'll help them to live a long and healthy life.

4) Poisonous Plants

Many common house plants are actually poisonous to our canine companions, and although many dogs simply will ignore house plants, some will attempt to eat anything, especially puppies who want to taste everything in their new world.

More than 700 plant species contain toxins that may harm or be fatal to puppies or dogs, depending on the size of the puppy or dog and how much they may eat. It will be especially important to be aware of household plants that could be toxic when you are sharing your home with a new puppy.

Below is a short list of the more common household plants, what they look like, the different names they are known by, and what symptoms would be apparent if your puppy or dog decides to eat them.

Aloe Plant: (medicine plant or Barbados aloe), is a very common succulent that is toxic to dogs. The toxic agent in this plant is Aloin.

This bitter yellow substance is found in most aloe species and may cause vomiting and/or reddish urine.

Asparagus Fern: (emerald feather, emerald fern, sprengeri fern, plumosa fern, lace fern). The toxic agent in this plant is sapogenin — a steroid found in a variety of plants. Berries of this plant cause vomiting, diarrhoea and/or abdominal pain or skin inflammation from repeated exposure.

Corn Plant: (cornstalk plant, dracaena, dragon tree, ribbon plant) is toxic to dogs. Saponin is the offensive chemical compound found in this plant. If the plant is eaten, vomiting (with or without blood), loss of appetite, depression and/or increased salivation can occur.

Cyclamen: (Sowbread) is a pretty, flowering plant that, if eaten, can cause increased salivation, vomiting and diarrhoea. If a dog eats a large amount of the plant's tubers, which are usually found below the soil at the root — heart rhythm abnormalities, seizures and even death can occur.

Dieffenbachia: (dumb cane, tropic snow, exotica) contains a chemical that is a poisonous deterrent to animals. If the plant is eaten, oral irritation can occur, especially on the tongue and lips. This irritation can lead to increased salivation, difficulty swallowing and vomiting.

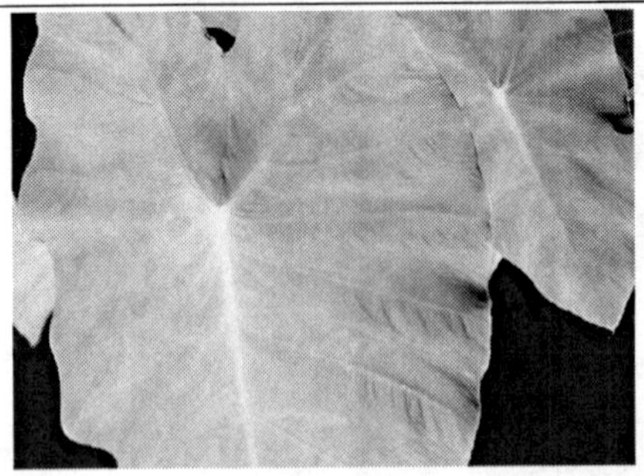

Elephant Ear: (caladium, taro, pai, ape, cape, via, via sori, malanga) contains a chemical similar to that found in dieffenbachia, therefore, a dog's toxic reaction to elephant ear is similar: oral irritation, increased salivation, difficulty swallowing and vomiting.

Heartleaf Philodendron: (horsehead philodendron, cordatum, fiddle leaf, panda plant, split-leaf philodendron, fruit salad plant, red emerald, red princess, saddle leaf), is a common, easy-to-grow houseplant that contains a chemical irritating to the mouth, tongue and lips of dogs. An affected dog may also experience increased salivation, vomiting and difficulty swallowing.

Jade Plant: (baby jade, dwarf rubber plant, jade tree, Chinese rubber plant, Japanese rubber plant, friendship tree). While the toxic property in this plant is unknown, eating it can cause depression, loss of coordination and, although more rare, slow heart rate.

Lilies: some plants of the lily family are toxic to dogs. The peace lily (also known as Mauna Loa) is toxic to dogs. Eating the peace lily or calla lily can cause irritation of the tongue and lips, increased salivation, difficulty swallowing and vomiting.

Satin Pothos: (silk pothos), if eaten by a dog, the plant may cause irritation to the mouth, lips and tongue, while the dog may also experience increased salivation, vomiting and/or difficulty swallowing.

The plants noted above are only a few of the more common household plants, and every conscientious Kangal guardian will want to educate themselves before bringing plants into the home that could be toxic to their canine companions.

5) Poison Proof Your Home

You can learn about many potentially toxic and poisonous sources both inside and outside your home by visiting the ASPCA Animal Poison Control Centre website.

Always keep your veterinarian's emergency number in a place where you can quickly access it, as well as the Emergency Poison Control telephone number, in case you suspect that your dog may have been poisoned.

Knowing what to do if you suspect your dog may have been poisoned and being able to quickly contact the right people could save your dog's life.

If you keep toxic cleaning substances (including fertilizers, vermin or snail poisons and vehicle products) in your home or garage, always keep them behind closed doors.

Keep any medications where your dog can never get to them, and seriously consider eliminating the use of any and all toxic products, for the health of both yourself and your best friend.

6) Garden Plants

Please note that there are also many outdoor plants that can be toxic or poisonous to your dog, therefore, always check what plants are growing in your garden and if any may be harmful, remove them or make certain that your Kangal puppy or adult dog cannot eat them.

Cornell University, Department of Animal Science lists many different categories of poisonous plants affecting dogs, including house plants, flower garden plants, vegetable garden plants, plants found in swamps or moist areas, plants found in fields, trees and shrubs, plants found in wooded areas, and ornamental plants.

7) Why Does My Dog Eat Grass?

Also be aware that many puppies and adult dogs will eat grass, just because. Perhaps they are curious, bored, or need a little fibre in their diet.

Remember that canines are natural scavengers, always on the look out for something they can eat, and so long as the grass is healthy and has not been sprayed with toxic chemicals, this should not be a concern.

8) Animal Poison Control centre

The ASPCA Animal Poison Control Centre is staffed 24 hours a day, 365 days a year and is a valuable resource for learning about what plants are toxic and possibly poisonous to your dog.

USA Poison Emergency

Call: 1 (888) 426-4435

When calling the Poison Emergency number, a $65. US (£39.42) consultation fee may be applied to your credit card.

UK Poison Emergency

Call: 0800-213-6680 - Pet Poison Helpline (payable service)

Call: 0300 1234 999 - RSPCA

www.aspca.org = ASPCA Poison Control.

Chapter 11: Financial Aspects of Getting a Kangal Dog

The Kangal dog is an expensive breed – from all aspects. Their acquisition costs are quite high, ranging up to several thousands. At the same time, their constant upkeep and maintenance also incur additional costs. If you are looking for a realistic estimate, here it is.

Prior owners of Kangal dogs observe that their pet consumes, on the average, about $420 to $780 / £244 £455 to of their yearly budget. This estimate is the lowest possible that you need to spend on your Kangal dog's upkeep. If you try to be a "giving" master, you can expect these figures to skyrocket to colossal heights.

a. Cost of Edibles

The primary cost in this figure is the cost of its food – an expense that you need to make in all cases. Kangal dogs need high quality dry dog food. If you try to put them on people food, they are likely to develop health problems that will end up costing you significantly more than the amount you saved on dog food.

The best ones on the market cost between $40 / £23 and $70 / £40 for a 27-30 pound bag. Depending on the size of your Kangal dog, this may last a month (if it weighs about 50lbs and consumes roughly 1 pound of food daily) to 10 days (if it weighs about 160 lbs and consumes about 3 pounds of food daily). Simple maths can show you how significant this cost amounts up to over the months.

Moreover, this does not include the cost of treats and other supplements you might decide to give to your pet. The treats alone can incur an additional cost up to $20 / £12 for a bag. Vitamins and other supplements may have varying costs depending on their composition ranging between $10 / £6 and $250 £145 per bottle. Generally, you do not need to worry about vitamins and supplements if you have a puppy. The same, however, cannot be said for the aged Kangal dogs.

When it is about taking care of your pet, the sky is the only limit about what it may cost you.

b. Dog Accessories

The estimate mentioned above does not include the cost of dog accessories like the travel crate, dog toys and other items of use. Usually these are purchased well in advance and can be used for years at a stretch.

If you are still looking for an estimate, consider this; an average travel crate for your Kangal can cost between $120 / £70 and $200 / £116. However, if you settle for a smaller travel crate to accommodate a Kangal puppy, you will need to buy another one as the puppy grows rapidly into its larger-than-life adulthood. Intelligent choices can save you quite a bit.

As far as its grooming is concerned, be ready to spend another couple of hundreds on these accessories. For instance, you can get nail clippers and trimmers for $20 / £11 to $60 / £35. A regular hairbrush can cost you about $15 / £8 but if you go for de-shedding tools, they may cost up to $60 / £35. Pet wipes may cost about $20 per pack and medicated shampoos can cost you about the same. If you purchase them all, you may incur a cost of $100 / £58 or more on grooming supplies alone.

Collars and leashes are another important expense that can cost you anything between $10 (for the most basic accessory) to $70 (for more stylish equipment with multiple utility). If you decide to add in a couple of flashy identification tags to the collar, you can add in a few more bucks to compensate for that. The purpose served by the $10 leash will be more or less the same as that of the $70 one. The only difference is that the latter might offer you options to "fasten" your pet into your car as well.

Dog toys are relatively inexpensive. You can get a bunch of these for $10 and they would be durable enough to last six months if not one year. If you go for stuffed toys, the cost may be slightly higher – about $15 for a toy. Nevertheless, these costs are very well justified and contribute a small portion of your overall expenses.

c. The Veterinarian

Your concerns don't end here. There is the annual trip to the veterinary doctor as well that is bound to gouge a significant hole in your financial resources.

It largely depends on the locality you live in. In some places, you can find veterinary services for much cheaper than in other places. On the whole, it can cost you about $250 to $1,000 / £145 to £582. If you are looking for specialized services like micro chipping, the costs will be significant and charged separately. Any other surgical procedures that your pet needs will incur costs over the given estimate.

The annual check-up costs tend to be larger for two reasons – firstly, you are not making a payment out of your pocket every month; secondly, this cost generally includes the expenses pertaining to blood tests, heartworm tests and several other similar examinations. The cost of yearly vaccinations is also embedded in this cost. Hence the mountainous amount is justified.

Alternatively, if you go for semi-annual check-ups, it will cost you about $100 to $150 / £58 to £101 per visit. The scarcity of such services has contributed towards selective inflation in this segment of medical care. Make sure you check in with your preferred veterinarian beforehand to get a realistic estimate of your yearly budget.

If you settle for a diseased puppy or a disease-prone breed, rest assured your medical care costs will be significantly higher than those mentioned in here. This is also one of the reasons why purchasing registered dogs from authentic breeders is encouraged.

Additionally, the cost of spaying or neutering a Kangal dog is also quite high. If you want to get a female Kangal spayed, it will cost you between $170 and $240 / £99 and £140. The cost of neutering male Kangal dogs range between $120 and $175 / £70 and £101. This is a onetime expenditure and hence should not be a major concern for you. You can also find non-profit charitable organizations in your vicinity to help take care of your pet if the costs are getting too high beyond affordability.

d. Pet Insurance

Pet owners commonly ask themselves, when considering medical insurance for their dog, whether they can afford not to have it.

On the one hand, in light of all the new treatments and medications that are now available for our dogs, that usually come with a very high price tag, an increasing number of guardians have decided to add pet insurance to their list of monthly expenses.

On the other hand, some people believe that placing money into a savings account, in case unforeseen medical treatments are required, makes more sense.

Pet insurance coverage can cost anywhere from $2,000 to $6,000 USD (£1201 to £3604) over an average lifespan of a dog, and unless your dog is involved in a serious accident, or contracts a life-threatening disease, you may never need to pay out that much for treatment.

Whether you decide to start a savings account for your Kangal dog so that you will always have funds available for unforeseen health issues, or you decide to buy a health insurance plan, most dog lovers will go to any lengths to save the life of their beloved companions.

Having access to advanced technological tools and procedures means that our dogs are now being offered treatment options that were once only reserved for humans.

Now, some canine conditions that were once considered fatal, are being treated at considerable costs ranging anywhere between $1,000 and $5,000 (£597 and £2,986) or more.

However, even in the face of rapidly increasing costs of caring for our dogs, owners purchasing pet insurance remain a small minority.

In an effort to increase the numbers of people buying pet insurance, insurers have teamed with the American Kennel Club and Petco Animal Supplies to offer the insurance, and more than 1,600 companies, such as Office Depot and Google, offer pet insurance coverage to their employees as an optional employee benefit.

Even though you might believe that pet insurance will be your saviour anytime your dog needs a trip to the vet's office, you really need to be careful when considering an insurance plan, because there are many policies that contain small print excluding certain ages, hereditary or chronic conditions.

Unfortunately, most people don't consider pet insurance when their pets are healthy because buying pet insurance means playing the odds, and unless your dog becomes seriously ill, you end up paying for something that may never happen.

However, just like automobile insurance, you can't buy it after you've had that accident.

Therefore, since many of us, in today's uncertain economy, may be hard pressed to pay a high veterinarian bill, generally speaking, the alternative of paying monthly pet insurance premiums will provide peace of mind and improved veterinarian care for our best friends.

Shop around, because as with all insurance policies, pet insurance policies will vary greatly between companies and the only way to know for certain exactly what sort of coverage you are buying is to be holding a copy of that policy in your hand so that you can clearly read what will and what will not be covered.

Don't forget to carefully read the fine print to avoid any nasty surprises, because the time to discover that a certain procedure will not be covered is not when you are in the middle of filing a claim.

There are several considerations to be aware of before choosing to purchase a pet insurance policy. This includes:

1. Is your dog required to undergo a physical exam?
2. Is there a waiting period before the policy becomes active?
3. What percentage of the bill does the insurance company pay — after the deductible?

4. Are payments limited or capped in any way?
5. Are there co-pays (cost to you up front)?
6. Does the plan cover pre-existing conditions?
7. Does the plan cover chronic or recurring medical problems?
8. Can you choose any vet or animal hospital to treat your pet?
9. Are prescription medications covered?
10. Are you covered when travelling with your pet?
11. Does the policy pay if your pet is being treated and then dies?

When you love your dog and worry that you may not have the funds to cover an emergency medical situation that could unexpectedly cost thousands, the right pet insurance policy will provide both peace of mind and better health care for your beloved canine friend.

e. Dog Training

This brings us to another important financial aspect to petting a Kangal dog – the cost of training. This also depends on your locality and if you are lucky you might be able to find certain resources that are more affordable.

On average, a single training class with the training centre can cost you between $15 and $45 / £8 and £26. Group classes average from $150 to $250 / £87 to £145 for a four to six week schedule respectively. The twist here is this; there are more than a dozen training courses for dogs. Each training course comes at a price. So if you add it all up, you will end up with a figure that may be out of reach.

For this reason, conducting a needs assessment beforehand will be a good option. As an owner, you have the right kind of experience to understand what kind of training your pet needs. Consequently, you can work in collaboration with your local training centres to work on those areas that demand attention. Getting your pet to behave well is definitely a priority compared to having your pet fetch various things on your order.

If you are unclear about what type of training classes your pet needs in order to improve its responses, you can consult and discuss it with training experts available at the centre. They will guide you through the process in the best possible manner while making sure the results you seek are delivered.

e. Miscellaneous Expenses

There are a few other dog accessories – like dog gates, barriers and other similar installations – for which an estimate has not been included deliberately. It all depends on you – how much you are willing to spend. The more you spend, the more accessories your pet will have. Even though this does not always translate into its happiness, it does mean exaggerated comfort for your beloved canine friend.

Apart from all these costs, you should be prepared for property damage as well when and if the Kangal dog becomes too agitated to calm down. It can wreak havoc in your living space, tear up the sofas and curtains and is very well equipped to knock down your doors too. Usually training does the trick but it pays to be safe and anticipate the worst even if it isn't happening.

Usually, the first year is the hardest and the most expensive. This is the time when your pet is settling in and is therefore going through a number of adjustment issues. So when and if it tries to express its anger or frustration, it can end up costing you a couple of dollars. However, over time, your pet will learn to respect your authority and will therefore make things much easier.

All the figures given in here are estimates. Actual prices of commodities may vary. A range has been given to accommodate the expensive as well as inexpensive options.

In fact, the yearly estimates given above also pertain to situations where you keep away from unnecessary and luxurious expenditures. The more you try to pamper your pet, the higher the total costs will become. Even though your pet does not really understand "money" as much as it understands "love", it will nevertheless like being pampered. For Kangal dogs, their luxury threshold is reached sooner than most other breeds.

Keeping and maintaining a Kangal dog is by no means an easy feat. It does not only demand a significant portion of your finances but also an equally exhaustive slice of your time and effort. There is a lot you need to do to make this association work out positively. Although the Kangal dog is an intelligent learner, it nevertheless will not be able to understand your rules if you do not make a conscious effort to get the right message across.

So do you really have it in you to pet a Kangal dog and also provide nothing but the best for it?

Chapter 12: General Tips and Tricks

Here are some general tips and tricks that will come in handy while caring for your Kangal dog (or any other dog for that matter).

1) First Weeks With Your Puppy

a) The First Night

Before you go to the breeder's to pick up your new Kangal puppy, vacuum your floors, including all the dust bunnies under the bed.

Do a last minute check of every room to make sure that everything that could be a puppy hazard is carefully tucked away out of sight and that nothing is left on the floor or low down on shelves where a curious puppy might get into trouble.

Close most of the doors inside your home, so that there are just one or two rooms that the puppy will have access to.

You have already been shopping and have everything you need, so get out a puppy pee pad and have it at the ready when you bring your new fur friend home.

Also have your soft bed(s) in an area where you will be spending most of your time and where your puppy can easily find them.

If you have already purchased a soft toy, take the toy with you when you go to pick up your puppy.

NOTE: take either your hard-sided kennel or your soft-sided "Sherpa" travel bag (lined with pee pads) with you when going to bring your new puppy home, and make sure that it is securely fastened to the seat of your vehicle with the seatbelt restraint system.

Even though you will be tempted to hold your new puppy in your lap on the drive home, this is a very dangerous place for them to be, in case of an accident.

Place them inside their kennel or bag, which will be lined with soft towels and perhaps even a warm, towel wrapped hot water bottle (and a pee pad), and close the door.

If you have a friend who can drive for you, sit beside your puppy in the back seat, and if they cry on the way home, remind them that they are not alone with your soft, soothing voice.

Before bringing your new puppy inside your home, take them to the place where you want them to relieve themselves and try to wait it out long enough for them to at least go pee.

Then bring them inside your home and introduce them to the area where their food and water bowls will be kept, in case they are hungry or thirsty.

Let your puppy wander around sniffing and checking out their new surroundings and encourage them to follow you wherever you go.

Show them where the puppy pee pad is located and place it near the door where you will exit to take them outside to go potty.

Many pee pads are scented to encourage a puppy to pee, and if they do, happily praise them.

Show them where their hard-sided kennel is and put them inside with the door open while you sit on the floor in front and quietly encourage them to relax inside their kennel.

Depending on the time of day when you bring your new Kangal puppy home for the first time, practice this kennel exercise several times throughout the day, and if they will take a little treat each time you encourage them to go inside their kennel, this will help to further encourage the behaviour of them wanting to go inside.

After they have had their evening meal, take them outside approximately 20 minutes later to go to the bathroom, and when they do, make sure you are very enthusiastic with your praise and perhaps even give a little treat.

So far your puppy has only been allowed in several rooms of your home, as you have kept the other doors closed, so keep it this way for the first few days.

Before it's time for bed, again take your puppy outside for a very short walk to the same place where they last went potty and make sure that they go pee before bringing them back inside.

Before bed, prepare your puppy's hot water bottle and wrap it in a towel so that it will not be too hot for them, and place it inside their hard-sided kennel.

Turn the lights down low and invite your puppy to go inside their kennel and if they seem interested, perhaps give them a soft toy to have inside with them. Let them walk into the kennel under their own steam and when they do, give them a little treat (if they are interested) and encourage them to snuggle down to sleep while you are sitting on the floor in front of the kennel.

Once they have settled down inside their kennel, close the door, go to your bed and turn all the lights off. It may help your puppy to sleep during their first night home, if you can play quiet, soothing music in the background.

If they start to cry or whine, stay calm and have compassion because this is the first time in their young life when they do not have the comfort of their mother or their litter mates.

Do not let them out of their kennel if they are crying, but rather, simply reassure them with your calm voice that they are not alone until they fall asleep.

TIP: if your bed is wide enough to accommodate your puppy's kennel, it may help them to fall asleep for the first few nights in their new kennel, if you have it beside you on top of the bed, so that you are closer to them. If there is any danger of the kennel falling off the bed during the night, do NOT do this as you will traumatize your puppy and make them afraid of their kennel.

b) The First Week

During the first week, you and your new puppy will be getting settled into their new routine, which will involve you getting used to your puppy's needs as they also get used to your usual schedule.

Be as consistent as possible with your waking and sleeping routine, getting up and going to bed at the same time each day, so that it will be easier for your puppy to get into the flow and routine of their new life.

First thing in the morning, remove your puppy from their kennel and take them immediately outside to relieve themselves at the place where they last went pee.

At this time, if you are teaching them to ring a doorbell to go outside, let them ring the bell before you go out the door with them, whether you are carrying them, or whether they are walking out the door on their own.

NOTE: during the first week, you may want to carry your puppy outside first thing in the morning as they may not be able to hold it for very long once waking up.

When you bring them back inside, you can let them follow you so they get used to their new leash and/or harness arrangement.

Be very careful not to drag your puppy if they stop or pull back on the leash.

TIP: if they refuse to walk on the leash, just hold the tension towards you (without pulling) while encouraging them to walk towards you, until they start to move forward again.

Now it will be time for their first feed of the day, and after they have finished eating, keep an eye on the clock, because you will want to take them outside to relieve themselves in about 20 minutes.

When your puppy is not eating or napping, they will be wanting to explore and have little play sessions with you and these times will help you bond with your puppy more and more each day.

As their new guardian, it will be your responsibility to keep a close eye on them throughout the day, so that you can notice when they need to relieve themselves and either take them to their pee pad or take them outside.

You will also need to make sure that they are eating and drinking enough throughout the day, so set regular feeding times at least three times a day.

Also set specific times in the day when you will take your puppy out for a little walk on a leash and harness, so that they are not only going outside when they need to relieve themselves, but they are also learning to explore their new neighbourhood with you beside them.

When your puppy is still very young, you will not want to walk for a long time as they will get tired easily, so keep your walks to no more than 15 or 20 minutes during your first week and if they seem tired or cold, pick them up and carry them home.

2) What You Should and Should Not Be Doing

Here are some of the common mistakes made by people while petting their canine companions.

Make sure you are not one of them as this can seriously disrupt your relationship with your Kangal dog at some point in time or the other.

a. Experimentation

First and foremost, you should not experiment with your pet, especially in matters pertaining to its health.

Self-medication is the last thing you should do even if your pet seems to have developed a problem that had occurred previously. You might be inclined to do so in order to save some costs but do keep in mind the dog doesn't respond to medication in the same way as humans.

If and when your plan backfires, the results will be even more drastic.

b. Sleeping in Your Bed

Many of us humans make the mistake of allowing a crying puppy to sleep in their bed, and while this may help to calm and comfort a new puppy, it will set a dangerous precedent that can result in behavioural problems later in their life.

As much as it may pull on your heart strings to hear your new Kangal puppy crying the first couple of night in their kennel, a little tough love at the beginning will keep them safe while helping them to learn to both love and respect you as their leader.

c. Picking Them Up at the Wrong Time

Never pick your puppy up if they display nervousness, fear or aggression (such as growling) towards an object, person or other pet, because this will be rewarding them for unbalanced behaviour.

Instead, your puppy needs to be gently corrected by you, with firm and calm energy so that they learn not to react with fear or aggression.

d. Playing Too Hard or Too Long

Many humans play too hard or allow their children to play too long or too roughly with a young puppy.

You need to remember that a young puppy tires very easily and especially during the critical growing phases of their young life, they need their rest.

e. Hand Play

Always discourage your Kangal puppy from chewing or biting your hands, or any part of your body for that matter.

If you allow them to do this when they are puppies, they will want to continue to do so when they have strong jaws and adult teeth and this is not acceptable behaviour for any breed of dog.

Do not get into the habit of playing the "hand" game, where you rough up the puppy and slide them across the floor with your hands, because this will teach your puppy that your hands are playthings.

When your puppy is teething, they will naturally want to chew on everything within reach, and this will include you. As cute as you might think it is, this is not acceptable behaviour and you need to gently, but firmly, discourage the habit.

A light flick with a finger on the end of a puppy nose, combined with a firm "NO" when they are trying to bite human fingers will discourage them from this activity.

f. Not Getting Used to Grooming

Not taking the time to get your Kangal used to a regular grooming routine, including bathing, brushing, toenail clipping and teeth brushing can lead to a lifetime of trauma for both human and dog every time these procedures must be performed.

Set aside a few minutes each day for your grooming routine.

Get your Kangal used to being up high, on a table or countertop when you are grooming them, because when it comes time for a full grooming session, then they will not be stressed by being placed on a grooming table.

g. Free Feeding

Free feeding means to keep food in your puppy's bowl 24/7 so that they can eat any time of the day or night, whenever they feel like it.

While free feeding a young puppy can be a good idea until they are about four or five months old, many guardians of different breeds often get into the bad habit of allowing their adult dogs to continue to eat food any time they want, by leaving food out 24/7.

This can be a serious mistake, as your Kangal needs to know that you are absolutely in control of their food.

If your Kangal does not associate the food they eat with you, they may become picky eaters or think that they are the bosses, which can lead to other behavioural issues later in life.

So be intelligent about your Kangal decision right from the beginning. You are about to create a rewarding relationship with your pet – don't spoil it by making the wrong decisions right at the start.

h. Extraordinary Creation

You should not consider it as an extraordinary being of any sort. It cannot take care of itself, cannot recognize what may be lethal for it and definitely cannot be expected to adapt or adjust to different settings.

It is not human, and you being its owner are responsible for keeping it healthy. Don't be negligent about your pet's needs – you never know when you might end up harming your own pal.

i. Being Too Distracted

If you have too many distractions to keep you busy through days or nights, are planning to have a child of your own, are one of the laid back types or simply cannot devote time and attention to your pet for whatever reason, it is best to stay away from such a commitment.

Kangal dogs demand more effort as compared to other breeds. If you cannot keep up with its pace, well then don't get involved.

j. No Need for Training

Besides this, never be misled into believing your Kangal dog is naturally well behaved or does not need training because it seems to be doing very well without it.

Kangal dogs learn quickly and will therefore follow your orders easily. However, it wouldn't be long before its internal state of crisis will get into the way of obedience.

Start training the Kangal dog as early as possible to make sure that unfortunate occurrences can be kept to a bare minimum.

The more you delay training for your Kangal dog, the more stubborn and irresponsive it will become. So it is in your best interest not to procrastinate this duty.

k. Inconsistent Orders

On the same note, make sure you (and your family) use consistent words for specific actions.

Your Kangal is not a human and will therefore become extremely confused if you use the same word and expect it to act differently.

Even if it is impulsively and linguistically right, the same cannot be said for your pet's understanding.

Consider this for example; if you want it to sit on the floor, you say "down" and when your spouse wants it off the sofa, they say "down". It will become worse when your kid says "down" to get the Kangal dog down a flight of stairs.

Linguistically, the word is used correctly in all three situations. But it is creating confusion in the mind of the Kangal about what the owner(s) wants.

It is best to use separate words for different actions and then reinforce this definition to make sure your Kangal dog respond well.

l. Not Using Enough Treats

It is recommended to use treats often, especially during the training phase. It is easily the best way to reinforce actions and responses.

So whenever your pet follows your orders or responds to the most recent training class, treat it with some snacks. It will know when it is being praised and will therefore respond to make you happy.

m. Loosing Temper

What would you do if your Kangal dog fails to perform the way you want it to?

Whatever you do, don't shout, holler or physically hurt it. Your Kangal dog is not a puppet that will follow your orders perfectly every time.

Making mistakes every now and then is perfectly normal for this animal. It will take time and patience to train your Kangal dog and have it follow your wishes. It does not happen overnight.

So if you are under the impression that training sessions begin yielding results right away, clear the misconception before penalizing your pet.

n. Leaving your dog off the Leash

Never try to leave your Kangal dog off the leash until and unless you are absolutely sure it is well disciplined.

Although it is encouraged to conduct your training sessions in public areas or in places where numerous distractions exist, make sure you do so once your pet has understood the basics.

Training amidst distractions makes sure your pet responds to your orders in similar situations.

If you leave it off the leash before training sessions take effect, it is more likely to wander off to restricted territories, bite a few people or animals and get you into a lot of trouble that could have been avoided if you kept the leash intact.

o. Leaving it Unattended

Lastly and most importantly, don’t let your pet get lonely or leave it unsupervised for long time periods.

It is a disastrous combination that can result in all sorts of damage – to your property as well as your pet. A lonely Kangal is likely to experiment with different objects within the house. Such activities are not always uneventful.

Don’t leave it unsupervised in a place where known threats exist. For instance, don’t keep it locked in the car or leave it around a park without supervision. Such negligence may end up inflicting irreversible pain to your pet.

p. Expecting too much.

Don't expect too much from your pet in too little time. Patience and perseverance is the key to success. Let your Kangal dog settle in and absorb your rules – it will eventually get there. Haste can only make matters worse for you as well as for your newfound pet.

q. Understanding Its Body Language

It can prove to be a big mistake to automatically assume that if the dog is wagging its tail, it is doing so because it is happy and/or friendly.

When determining the dog's true intent or demeanour, you need to take into consideration the entire body posture of the dog because it is highly possible that a dog can be wagging its tail just before it decides to take an aggressive lunge towards you.

More important in determining the emotional state of a dog is the height or positioning of its tail.

For instance, a tail that is held parallel to the dog's back usually suggests that the dog is feeling relaxed, whereas if the tail is held stiffly vertical, this usually means that the dog is feeling aggressive or dominant.

A tail held much lower can mean that the dog is feeling stressed, afraid, submissive or unwell and if the tail is tucked underneath the dog's body, this is most often a sign that the dog is feeling fearful and threatened by another dog or person.

Paying attention to your dog's tail can help you to know when you need to step in and make some space between your dog and another dog.

Of course, different breeds naturally carry their tails at different heights, so you will need to take this into consideration when studying your dog's tail so that you get used to their particular signals.

In addition, the speed the tail is moving at will also give you an idea of the mental state of the dog because the speed of the wag usually indicates how excited a dog may be.

For instance, a slow, slightly swinging wag can often mean that the dog is tentative about greeting another dog, and this is more of a questioning type of wag, whereas a fast moving tail held high can mean that a dog is about to challenge or threaten another dog. Interestingly, two veterinarians at the University of Bari and a neuroscientist at the University of Trieste, in Italy, published a paper in which their research outlined that dogs' tails wagged more to their right side when they had positive feelings about a person or situation, and more to the left side when they were feeling negative.

While certainly a dog's tail can help us humans to understand how our dogs might be feeling, there are many other factors to take into consideration when determining your dog's state of mind.

Simply looking at the tail to gauge its mood is therefore not recommended!

3) Bonding With Your Dog

You will begin bonding with your Kangal puppy from the very first moment you bring them home from the breeders.

This is the time when your puppy will be the most upset and nervous, as they will no longer have the guidance, warmth and comfort of their mother or their other littermates, and you will need to take on the role of being your new puppy's centre of attention.

Be patient, kind and gentle with them as they are learning you are now their new centre of the universe.

Your daily interaction with your puppy during play sessions and especially your disciplined exercises, including going for walks on leash, and teaching commands and tricks, will all be wonderful bonding opportunities.

Do not make the mistake of thinking that *"bonding"* with your new puppy can only happen if you are playing or cuddling together, because the very best bonding happens when you are kindly teaching rules and boundaries, and this intelligent puppy will be most eager to learn.

4) Finding Dog Clubs in Your Vicinity

A simple Internet search will also reveal a lot to you that you might not have known already. Finding dog clubs in your vicinity should not be a problem since there are so many of them. The national ones enjoy international recognition and are unarguably reliable. The local ones are just as good. If you are living in the United States, the KDCA is a good place to start.

You can consult your veterinarian for more information. Other dog owners will also be able to help you connect with local and authentic dog clubs. Do not just restrict your association to companionship – let your pet outshine competition outside home as well.

Dog clubs all over the world host thousands of dog shows and competitions round the year. It gives an opportunity for you to showcase your pet and earn points for its capabilities. It gives you a chance to shine amidst all dog owners as a person who is not only passionate about the specific breed but also about the specific dog.

On the other hand, it gives you a chance to meet up with other dog enthusiasts and share your stories. You can come across pearls of wisdom during these exchanges that might help you ward off future trouble with your pet. It is always best to learn from those who "have been there and done that!"

You can also pinpoint areas where you may be going wrong. It is an opportunity to learn as well as to share. Make the most of it by selecting a dog club that meets your expectations. Most dog clubs do not have hefty membership fees – all the more reason to find one for yourself as well as your canine friend. In the end, it is an investment worth making.

5) Caring for Pregnant Females

A Kangal dog's pregnancy usually lasts for about 9 weeks or 63 days – a few days up or down. This is the time period where the mother needs to be cared for.

Usually, there will be no evident signs of pregnancy in the first month. It is during the second month when the bodily changes will begin to happen rather speedily. This is the most vulnerable time for the mother and hence needs utmost care.

It is advised not to have pregnant females doing any vigorous works. They should be kept in a secluded place away from commotion and other animals. The environment should be carefully regulated so that the Kangal does not feel too hot or too cold. Their feeding should be scheduled for twice a day and the food given to them should be rich in proteins. It is best not to disturb them during this phase.

The place where the mother is supposed to relieve her burden should be cleaned and disinfected. Birth is a painful procedure; make sure a veterinarian is on call just in case the going gets too complicated.

6) Caring for the New Born

Ideally, the newborns should not be separated from the mother or their fellow littermates until they have completed their second month (8 weeks). This is an important educational institution for them where unparalleled value exchange takes place.

During the birth phase, the newborns are delivered in a film called the placenta. It is a natural instinct for the Kangal mother to lick and consume this film to clean and dry its puppies. This film is also a good source of protein which eventually helps the mother lactate.

At least for a period of 15-20 days after birth, it is advised not to touch the young ones. Firstly, it is normal for the Kangal mother to be protective about her offspring. Moreover, the puppies are too small and fragile during this time period. It is best not to touch them or try to separate them from the mother.

For the first two weeks, the only food they receive is the milk from the mother (or artificially administered one from feeding bottles). After this time period, the puppies become stable enough to walk around and eat the food from food bowls. After 3 months they need to be weaned off and shifted to solid food.

In the first few weeks, the frequency of feeding is higher even though the aggregate amount of dog food consumed is not much. Subsequently, the frequency declines as the amount increases. An adult Kangal can consume up to three pounds of dog food at a time.

Besides this, regulating the environment and temperature for the young Kangal dogs is also important. All their needs should be fulfilled to keep them fit and healthy and to prevent incidence of diseases.

7) Caring for an Aging Dog

Their demands and needs are infinitely different. It is common to come across one if you are involved in rescuing the Kangal breed. Here are some of the things you need to keep in mind while handling aged Kangal dogs.

Aged Kangal dogs, especially if they come from battered homes, are likely to have several health issues. Make sure you keep these in mind while preparing their meals and activities.

It is advised not to serve them any hard foods or bones that can damage their gums. Also, keep the oil content in foods low so that digestive issues can be kept to a minimum.

On this note, keep in mind that some of the health problems faced by your Kangal dog are likely to come naturally with age. There is no way to delay or eliminate these.

For instance, most aged dogs will experience reduced hearing and sight. Learn to differentiate between imminent dangers and the natural course of life.

Your veterinary doctor is more skilled to tell you about the different signs likely to be exhibited by your pet. However, it pays to consider anything out of the ordinary as a potential threat for your pet's well being.

Aged Kangal dogs are not likely to be as energetic as young ones. Plan their activities in a placid manner.

Remember to take them out for walks and other activities as it helps prevent the arthritis from becoming a major problem.

Select a peaceful space in your house where they can rest through the day. You can take them for rides but beware of their stress urinary incontinence.

Don't forget the annual check-ups. Better still increase its frequency to semi-annually.

As far as the vaccinations are concerned, ask your veterinary doctor if it is advisable to tune down the frequency to once every three years.

Besides this, you might need to use some vitamins and supplements to counter failing health. The rest all should be fine.

8) Keeping Them "Involved"

An "unemployed" Kangal dog has the potential to turn your home upside down. This is possible because of their massive size and more so due to their strength and energy reserves. It is therefore in your best interest to keep the Kangal dog busy.

Entrust it with a responsibility – the Kangal breed loves being in-charge. Either make it guard something or have it look after other people in your home. Make sure you take it for long walks (a minimum of two hours) every day to limit its destructive instincts.

If possible, have more than one Kangal dog to keep each other company. Make sure you invest in socialization efforts adequately and in a timely manner. The earlier you start acclimatizing your pet to its environment; the better off it will be for them and for you.

9) Handling Assault Cases

Kangal dogs have extremely protective attitudes. They guard their flock with their lives. Even though not aggressive by nature, they can turn into attackers if attacked first. In fact, any skirmishes that the owner gets into can readily aggravate into a major medical emergency if the Kangal dog is left off the leash.

Adequate socialization can help prevent such incidents. Help your pet understand who is to be considered as a threat and who isn't. Invest ample amount of time socializing your Kangal for best results.

Even so, if an unpleasant incident takes place, don't lose your calm. Get the Kangal dog away from the site of the crime and have it locked away safely. Then tend to the injuries of the victim and pay the medical costs. Don't try to blame the event on the victim as anything you say or do may be held against you.

Make sure your Kangal dog's vaccinations are up-to-date, so the damage is minimal even in an assault case. Moreover, if you suspect major trouble, consult a professional lawyer immediately. Keep in mind that in the worst-case scenario your companion may be euthanized. So it is much better to be vigilant about your pet than to regret your negligence later on!

Caring for your pet is simple provided you know what you need to do and when. It usually comes with experience.

Chapter 13: Identifying and Finding Lost Dogs

1) Micro-Chipping

A microchip implant is a tiny integrated circuit, approximately twice the size of a large grain of rice, enclosed in glass that is implanted under the skin of a dog (or other animal) with a syringe.

The chip uses passive Radio Frequency Identification (RFID) technology, and is also known as a PIT tag (Passive Integrated Transponder).

The microchip is usually implanted, without anaesthetic, into the scruff of a dog's neck by a veterinarian or shelter.

The microchip has no internal power source, which means that they must be read by a scanner or *"interrogator"*, which energizes the capacitor in the chip, which then sends radio signals back to the scanner so that the identifying number can be read.

Manufacturers of microchips often donate scanners to animal shelters and veterinarian clinics and hospitals.

While many communities are proposing making micro-chipping of all dogs mandatory, such as N. Ireland, and micro-chipping is a requirements for any dogs travelling to the state of Hawaii, many others are not especially pleased with this idea because they believe it's just more big business for little reward.

For instance, while approximately one quarter of European dogs have a microchip implant, the idea is definitely lacking in popularity in the United States, where only 5% of dogs are micro-chipped.

Even though micro-chipping is used by animal shelters, pounds, animal control officers, breeders and veterinarians, in order to help return a higher percentage of lost canines to their owners, some of the resistance to this idea can be explained by inherent problems with the ability of some organizations to correctly read the implants.

As an example, if the scanner is not tuned to the same frequency as the implanted microchip, it will not be read, which renders the process useless.

Pet microchips are manufactured with different frequencies, including 125 kHz, 128 kHz and 134.2 kHz.

While approximately 98% of the pet microchips in the US use 125 kHz, those in Europe use 134.2 kHz.

In other words, if the facility reading your dog's microchip does not have a compatible scanner, your dog will not be identified and returned to you.

Furthermore, what may turn out to be worse than the scanner incompatibility problem could be increasing evidence to indicate that microchips might cause cancer.

Some microchips will migrate inside the dog's body and while they may start out in the dog's neck, they could end up in their leg or some other body part.

You will have to weigh-up information known about microchips, including possible cancer risks, and the odds of losing your dog against whether or not a microchip is something you want to have for your Kangal.

Whether or not you choose a microchip for your dog, generally the cost ranges between $25 and $50 (£15 and £30) depending on what your veterinarian may charge for this service.

2) Tattooing

Dogs are tattooed to help identify them in case they are lost or stolen and many dog guardians prefer this safe, simple solution to micro-chipping.

Tattooing does not require locating a scanner that reads the correct frequency and there are no known side effects.

Because a tattoo is visible, it is immediately recognizable and reported when a lost dog is found, which means that tattooing could easily be the most effective means of identification available.

Dog thieves are less likely to steal a dog that has a permanent visible form of identification. There are several registries for tattooed dogs, including the National Dog Tattoo Registry in the UK, which has a network of Accredited Tattooists across the UK.

The fee for tattooing and registering a dog for their lifetime is approximately £25 / £15.

In the United States, the National Dog Registry (NDR) was founded in 1966 and since then, NDR has supervised, directed, conducted, or overseen the tattooing of more than 6 million animals. The cost for tattooing a single dog is approximately $10 / £6, plus a one-time registration fee of $45 / £26.

3) Where to Look

If your Kangal goes missing, there are many places you can contact and steps you can take that may help you locate your lost dog, including:

- Retracing your dog's last known location;
- Contacting your friends and neighbours;
- Putting up flyers on telephone poles throughout your neighbourhood, with your contact details and a photograph of your dog;
- Calling all local shelters and pounds every day;
- Contacting local rescue organisations;
- Contacting your breeder;
- Contacting local schools - children might have seen your dog in their neighbourhood;
- Distributing flyers with a photograph of your dog and your contact details in all neighbourhood stores and businesses;
- Contacting all businesses that deal with lost pets;
- Posting a picture on your Facebook or other social media;
- Asking your local radio station for help;
- Advertising in your local newspaper.

Chapter 14: Checklists

List # 1:

	Preliminary Shopping List:
	Veterinarian has been selected.
	Food has been purchased and stocked (up to two weeks).
	Food and Water bowls are available.
	ID tags, collar and leash have been bought.
	It has a place to sleep in.
	It has something to keep it occupied.
	Travel arrangements have been made.
	It has something to wear – if it is winter.
	All necessary grooming supplies are available.
	Potty training equipment is stocked (at least until your pet learns to use the spot).

List # 2:

	Dog Proofing:
	There is a fence around your house.
	Safety latches are put on all cupboards.
	All doors are made to shut automatically.
	All wires are covered and shoved away.
	There are no small, fragile and potentially dangerous items in the living room.
	There is a pet door installed in the main door.
	The washroom doors are closed automatically.
	Unfriendly plants are cordoned off.
	Barriers have been placed strategically to avoid contact between the Kangal dog and dangerous items/areas/zones.
	There is an extra barrier available to be used while using chemicals for regular cleaning etc.
	Carpets have been installed in areas where the dog stays for extended periods of time.

List # 3:

The Feeding Calendar:		
	0 – 2 months	Mother's Feed Only (Ideally)
If separated before the right age:		
	0 – 2 weeks	400 ml of milk; 6 – 8 times a day
	2 – 4 weeks	300 ml of milk with biscuits; 4 – 6 times a day
	1 – 2 months	200 ml of milk with half a pound of solid food; 4 times in a day
	2 – 6 months	Half a pound of solid food; 3 times in a day.
	6 – 12 months	1 pound of solid food; 2 times in a day.
	12 months +	3 pound of solid food; once a day.

List # 4:

Real Age of the Kangal Dog:	
Birth	Born with eyes shut tightly. The average weight is about 500 to 600 grams
8 - 9 days	The weight doubles and reaches up to 1200 grams.
9 – 10 days	The Kangal dog opens the eyes slightly for the first time.
12 – 14 days	Eyes are now wide open and mischievously playful.
2 weeks	There are the first struggles to walk around the place and explore new things.
2 – 3 weeks	The ears are opened. By this time, the Kangal dog begins to consume food from the feeding bowls so their initial nursing period is over. Feeding from feeding bottles is also stopped at this point.
3 weeks	The puppy starts teething. Two of the upper canines and six of the upper incisors begin to show their first glimpses. The puppy becomes more active, starts to run, play and fight and may even start snarling at things that upsets it.
3 – 4 weeks	The Kangal becomes increasingly inquisitive about its surroundings and is likely to be seen exploring “distant lands”. The puppy begins to grow in size and the excessively fatty/chubby appearance begins to fade.
4 weeks	The lower jaw begins to fill in. 2 of the lower canines and 6 of the lower incisors begin to make their way into the limelight. The dog also learns how to bark.

5 weeks	The molars begin to emerge out of the skin. 8 molars become evident on the jaws.
6 weeks	It is time for the premolars. 4 of these emerge on the jaws.
7 weeks	The Kangal approaches maturity. It weighs about 5kgs and reaches up to a height of 30cms. It learns how to use its claws and teeth to gnaw at its food and consume it.
8 weeks	The milk diet is restrained. The Kangal dog is slowly transited to good quality low-protein dog food.
3 months	The puppy has become thrice as big as it was at birth and weighs almost 20 times as much as it did back then. The puppy is approaching maturity.

Rescue Organizations

When you are considering rescuing a specific breed of dog or puppy, the first place to start your search will be with your local breeders, shelters and rescue groups.

Shelters

Here you can expect to pay an adoption fee to cover the cost of spaying or neutering, but this will only be a small percentage of what you would pay a breeder, and you will be saving a life at the same time.

Online Resources

Sites such as Petango, Adopt A Pet and Pet Finder can be good places to begin your search.

Each of these online resources is a central gathering site for hundreds and hundreds of local shelters, humane societies and rescue groups.

Canine Clubs and Breeders

Another place to search will be hybrid clubs or breeders in your local area. These groups may have rescue dogs available.

Resources & References

The following resources and references are listed alphabetically within their specific category and include web addresses.

Poison Control
ASPCA Poison Control [aspca.org]
Poisonous Plants Affecting Dogs - Cornell University, Department of Animal Science [ansi.cornell.edu/plants/dogs/]

Breeders, Registries & Rescues

Adopt A Pet [adoptapet.com]
American Canine Hybrid Club [achclub.com]
Breeders Club [breedersclub.net]
Designer Dogs Kennel Club [thekennelclub.org.uk]
Greenfield Puppies [greenfieldpuppies.com]
International Designer Canine Registry®
[designercanineregistry.com]
National Dog Tattoo Register [dog-register.co.uk]
National Dog Registry [nationaldogregistry.com]
Petango [petango.com]
Pet Finder [petfinder.com]

Equipment, Supplies & Services

www.dogbowlforyourdog.com
www.modernpuppies.com
www.poochie-pets.net
www.removeurineodors.com
www.sleepypod.com
www.tellbell.com
www.thundershirt.com

Here are some of the websites that might help you get an additional insight into the Kangal dog's lifestyle and needs.

1. http://www.kangalclub.com/
2. http://cynology.freehomepage.com
3. http://en.wikipedia.org/wiki/Kangal_dog
4. http://www.dogbreedinfo.com
5. http://kangal.ca/
6. http://www.kangalkopegi.org
7. http://www.kangaldogsinternational.org
8. http://www.allaboutturkey.com
9. http://www.ukcdogs.com
10. http://www.shadowwingsfarm.com
11. http://www.the1alpacafarm.com
12. http://www.thekennelclub.org.uk
13. http://www.dog-breeds-101.com
14. http://animalcaretip.com
15. http://longlivepuppies.com

Conclusion

Kangal dogs are an impressive breed. They have the tendency to adapt to your needs perfectly and reciprocate your emotions. They are strong animals not only in terms of strength but also in terms of willpower. These large dogs are good to cuddle with and they are equally ferocious towards their enemies.

Kangal dogs can be a challenge to handle and train. At the same time, they have the ability to become a family member. They are intelligent, protective and make great companions. Their guardian instincts can be put to use to protect livestock. What more could you possibly ask for?

I hope you have enjoyed reading this book and I hope you will be as happy with your Kangal as I am with mine.

I wish you the best for your canine petting adventures!

Published by IMB Publishing 2014

CPSIA information can be obtained at www.ICGtesting.com
Printed in the USA
BVOW04s1751181114

375655BV00021B/377/P